Adolescence
and
Family Life Education

ADOLESCENCE AND FAMILY LIFE EDUCATION

N. Nagarajan

SHIPRA

ISBN: 978-81-7541-527-0

First Published in India in 2010

Adolescence and Family Life Education

Published by:
SHIPRA PUBLICATIONS
H.O.: LG 18-19, Pankaj Central Market, Patparganj,
I.P. Ext., Delhi-110092, Tel: 91-11-22235152, 22236152
Br.Off.115, Munish Plaza, 20, Ansari Road, Darya Ganj,
New Delhi-110002, Tel: 65946453
E-mail: info@shiprapublications.com
www.shiprapublications.com

Acknowledgement

I wish to express my very sincere thanks to the university grants commission, New Delhi for providing financial support to this major research project.

I express my gratitude to the professor and Head, Department of Adult & Continuing Education for the continuous support and encouragement at various stages of the Research project.

I wish to record my sense of gratitude to Dr. R. Rajan, Programme Coordinator, State Resource Centre (SRC), Dr. K. Devaraj, Programme Coordinator, SRC, Dr. T. Jayaraj, Social Scientist, Directorate of Family Welfare, Tamilnadu, Mrs. Nalini Rajendran, Project Officer, FPAI, Chennai, Dr. N.V.R. Kapali and Dr. V.P. Matheswaran, APAC project, Department of Adult and Continuing education for their valuable suggestions and advice to bring the Resource package of Self-Instructional modules for college students.

I am also thankful to Mr. Perumal and Mr. Veerappan, project fellows for their help for bringing out this publication.

Contents

1

Adolescence, Marriage and Family Life

Introduction

'Adolescence' has been defined as a stage among human beings where a lot of physiological as well as anatomical changes take place resulting in reproductive maturity in them. The associated sexual changes also bring in a lot of psychological/ emotional changes. A change is also noticeable in the social attitude. These physical changes demand a great deal of adjustment both socially and emotionally. These people also need a proper guidance, counseling and consolation. On the whole we can say that the age between 12-19 years among the female and between 15-19 years among the male can be treated as adolescent age. The age between 15 and 24 can be 'young people' as a term broadly treated as 'youth' covers both age groups (WHO/UNFPA/UNICEF statement, 1989). However, in reality, the period of Adolescence cannot be confined to denote a precise range of years and it can fall within either of these ranges. Sometimes, in a few cases even the age of 10 has also been considered Adolescence.

Today one fifth of world population is in between ages 10 and 19. In general, girls enter puberty between ages 8 and 13 while boys between 9 and 14. The WHO (1996) defined Adolescence as:

- Progression from appearance of secondary sex characteristics (puberty) to sexual and reproductive maturity;

- Development of adult mental processes and adult identity;
- Transition from social-economic dependence to relative independence.

Mahale (1987) defined Adolescence as a transition period from childhood to adulthood extending from the eleventh year to the twentieth year, thus encompassing the teenage years. Boys and girls enter the adolescent years as children and leave them as adults. It is during these years that young people mature and develop the ability to live their lives as autonomous persons. The major thrust of this state of life is physical maturation.

Kashyap (1993) described the developmental tasks of Adolescents as follows;

- *Acceptance of changes in body and physique:* The first and probably the most difficult developmental task for adolescents is the acceptance of their changes in body and physique as well as psychological repercussions. The emergence of adult sexual potency is a source of disturbance and anxiety and may push the young person into clandestine experimentation leading to an increase in promiscuity, teenage pregnancies and venereal disease.
- *Achieving a satisfying and socially accepted Masculine or Feminine role:* A young girl's response to pubertal changes depend upon her attitudes toward herself as a female, and her feeling about her identification figure, the mother, parents are the primary sex role models for their grouping children. Therefore, their understanding and respect for their own sex roles as well as each other's sex role play an important part in their children imbibing a correct concept of sex rules. Parent's own attitude towards their sex and their child rearing pattern will form the foundation of sex orientation in the life of child.

- *Locating oneself as a member of one's generation by developing more mature relations with one's age mates:* An adolescent is a time for social expansion and development, adolescents tend to center a great of their lives about the activities, interests and attitudes of their peers and the peer groups assume greater importance. The peer culture sets patterns for stacking their claim to adult pleasure of sinuousness. Nearly all adolescents desire acceptance in the eyes of their age-mates and will go to extreme lengths to gain and maintain such acceptance. Hence, selection of friends and extent of interactions with them can be a potential area of family conflict.
- *Achieving Emotional Independence of Parents:* Sociologists and psychologists have viewed adolescence as a key developmental period during which the adolescents seek greater autonomy.
- *Selecting and Preparing for an occupation and Economic Independence:* It is during adolescence that the young persons try to think and aspire towards his/her future career. In the fulfillment of this development task, the family plays as important role, as all the youth's aspirations, values and goals are indirectly influence by the family situation in which they were molded during the whole childhood period.
- *Preparing for Marriage and Family Life:* Nearly all marriages in India are arranged marriages, especially in the villages. Selection of the spouse is done by elders in the family and within the same caste or sub caste.
- *Establishing one's Identity as a socially responsible person:* A specific unique task of adolescence is the establishment of 'ego identity'. The family, especially the parents plays a major role in shaping the process. This is a period of strain in most families. As adolescents strive to establish their identity, and to emancipate themselves from their parents, the parents tend to feel that their children under value them and the adolescents believe that adults generally depreciate

teenagers. However, when parents accept themselves as they are, with all their weakness and stage of development without undue conflict or sensitivity, they set a pattern for a sort of self-acceptance in their children.

Keeping the seriousness faced by the society, the emphasis laid down at the International Conference on Population and Development (ICPD) held at Cairo in September, 1994 which endorsed a new strategy of mutually reinforcing linkages between population and development and the key to this new approach is the empowerment of women both as an end in itself as a vital factor in improving the quality of life of every one.

According to ICPD, the objectives should be:

- To achieve equality and equity based on harmonious partnership between men and women and enable women to realize their full potential.
- To ensure women's contribution to sustainable development through their involvement and participation in policy and decision making employment, production, education, health, science and technology, sports, culture, etc., as active decision makers, participants and beneficiaries.
- To ensure that all women and men are provided with the education necessary for them to fulfill their basic human needs and to exercise their human rights.

By the way of action to achieve the above objectives, the following have been suggested in the programme of action of ICPD.

- Equal participation and equitable representation in the political process.
- Fulfillment of women's potential through education and skill development.
- Elimination of all discriminatory practices against

women especially with regard to their reproductive and sexual rights.

- Empowerment in women's ability to take-up non-traditional income generating activities.
- Elimination of violence against women.
- Introduction of legislation or regulations to combine women's reproductive and productive roles. Introduction of policies do enable both men and women to balance their family and work responsibilities through flexible working hours, parental leave, day care facilities and time off to breast feed etc.
- Equality in property rights, inheritance and access to credit.
- Elimination of gender discrimination in hiring, wages, benefits, training and job security.
- Equitable representation of women at policy and managerial levels.
- Gender based analysis of development programmes, gender audit and gender sensitive indicators to monitor and evaluate projects.
- Eliminating trafficking in women, adolescents and children and eliminating exploitation through prostitutions.
- Expansion and strengthening of grass roots, community based an activist groups of women.
- Progrmmes to meet the need of growing number of elderly, especially women.

In direction of empowering women, the ICPD programme of action has created a separate section on the girl child with following objectives:

- Elimination of all forms of discrimination against the girl child and the root cause of son preference, which results in harmful and unethical practices regarding female infanticide and pre-natal sex selection.
- To increase public awareness of the value of girl child

and strengthen girl child's self image, self-esteem and status.

- To improve the welfare of girl child, especially in regard to health, nutrition and education.

In support to the above objectives the ICPD suggests the following actions:

- Advocacy regarding the value of girl children and their potential as builders of society in equal measures with their brothers addressed to their families and to society.
- Elimination of gender discrimination within the family, especially with regards to education, nutrition, health care and equitable inheritance rights.
- Elimination of stereo types that project inequalities and lowers a girl's self-esteem in the education system the media and other social institutions.
- Laws to ensure that marriage is entered into only with the free will of both spouses and minimum age at marriage is pegged at a reasonable level and enforced.
- Stringent measures to represent female infanticide, sex selective abortions, trafficking and use of girls in prostitution and pornography.

It is now accepted fact that if we really interested in women empowerment, the attitude, knowledge and behaviour of both men and women would need a change. Men play a key role in bringing about gender equity and in most societies exercise preponderant power in every sphere of life. Thus, the above ICPD programme of action refers to a new paradigm shift of population and development.

The adolescents are going to enter in reproductive phase. They have to take the responsibility of parenthood in future. The sex education during adolescent age has its own advantage in their lives. Keeping the above recommendations made in the ICPD. In view, it was found worthwhile to conduct and exploratory study of adolescent learners to find out their existing knowledge and behariours regarding the issues of

List of Tables and Figures

LIST OF TABLES

LIST OF FIGURES

PART I

population education. The findings of this study would be used in planning the further training programmes and preparation of materials for them.

In the present study, knowledge, attitude and behaviour patterns of adolescent learners with regard to gender equality, women empowerment, and reproductive health including STDs and AIDS and Adolescent Behaviors have been studied.

Reproductive Health

The concept of Reproductive Health has been defined in ICPD programme of action which reads as 'Reproductive Health is a state of complete physical, mental and social well-being and not merely absence of disease or infirmity, in all matters related to the reproductive system and to its functions and processes'. Reproductive Health therefore, implies that people are able to have a satisfying and safe sex life and they have capability to reproduce and the freedom to decide if, when and how often to do so. Implicit in this last conditions are the rights of men and women to be informed and to have access to safe effective, affordable and acceptable methods of family planning of their choice as well as other methods of their choice for regulation of fertility which are not against the law and the right of access to appropriate health care services that will enable women to go safely through pregnancy and childbirth and provide couples with best chance of having a healthy infant. If also includes sexual health the purpose of which is enhancement of life and personal relations and not merely counseling and care related to reproduction and sexually transmitted diseases.

The Reproductive health programmes include the following essential components;

- Prevention of unintended pregnancy through the provision of accessible and high quality family planning services which are based on the reproductive health needs of couples.
- Provision of safe abortion and post abortion care services.

- Provision of safe motherhood services to improve maternal morbidity and mortality including services to improve prenatal, neonatal and post neonatal mortality.
- Prevention and treatment of reproductive tract infections and sexually transmitted diseases (STDs) and HIV/AIDS transmission.
- Provision of reproductive health services to adolescents.
- Improvement of maternal and infant including promotion of breast feeding.
- Screening and management of specific gynecological problems such as reproductive tract cancer and infertility.
- Addressing social problems such as, prevention and management of harmful practices, like female genital mutilation and gender based violence.

The life span approach to reproductive health begins with the birth of the baby, does not ignore early childhood, intensifies during adolescence and covers the reproductive health, brings a new dimension to safe motherhood, family planning and STD programmes. Integrating them, so that they are not delivered in isolation, enables communities to deal in a more comprehensive manner in order to overcome the issue of territoriality.

Reproductive Rights

First time in 1968 reproductive rights were recognized as human rights and were endorsed and strengthen in successive international for a, particularly at the 1994 ICPD at Cairo as well as at the Fourth World Conference on women in 1995 at Beijing. The Reproductive rights include the following key components;

- Reproductive and sexual health: as a component of overall health throughout the life cycle.

- Reproductive decision making: including voluntary choice in marriage, family formation and determination of the number, timing and spacing of one's children and the right to have access to the information and means needed to exercise voluntary choice.
- Equality and Equity for men and women: to enable individuals to make free and informed choices in all spheres of life, free from discrimination based on gender.
- Sexual and Reproductive security: including freedom from sexual violence and the right to privacy.

South Asia conference on Adolescence, New Delhi, 1988, the country paper indicates several issues that concerns adolescents.

- Girls still marry at a younger age although the mean age at marriage has risen to 20 years as compared to 24 for boys.
- 50 per cent of the girls aged 15-19 are already married resulting in early conception and high risks of maternal mortality.
- Increasing evidence of premarital sexual activity among educated Adolescents.
- Increasing incidence of illegal abortion and maternal deaths associate with premarital sex and early marriage. Around 12 per cent of the spontaneous abortions were reported among adolescents 13-14 years and 9 per cent among adolescents 15-19 years, including induced abortions.
- Increasingly, adolescents are exposed to non-pregnancy related reproductive health disorders such as STDs and STIs. Girls disproportionately affected.
- WHO estimates as may as 2.5 million Indians are infected with the HIV virus as of 1994, with 8,00,000 reported cases of AIDS. It is suspected that many Indians acquired the virus during adolescence.

- The incidence of adolescent rape (between 10-16 years age) increased by 26 per cent between 1991 and 1995. Alcohol abuse, in both domestic and non-domestic steins, appears to be main cause of adolescent rape.
- An insidious spread of drug use and addiction among those in the 12-23 years age group.
- Commercial sexual exploitation of children and young girls, including forced prostitution and trafficking is a serious and growing problem.

The reproductive health needs of adolescents as a group have been largely ignored to date by existing reproductive health services. It is required that information and services should be made available to adolescents to help them understand their sexuality and protect them from unwanted pregnancies, STDs and subsequent risk of infertility in short, the reproductive health needs of adolescents have not yet been seriously considered by either Government or Municipal authorities or NGOs.

After the International Conference on population and Development (ICPD) at Cairo, 1994 and the Beijing conference on Women and Development, 1995 elaborate discussions were made population, development and gender related issues which brought forth worldwide support and concern to address specially the adolescent's issues and needs.

There is scant provision of information, education and counseling the health needs of adolescents and young adults in our country with specific reference to sexuality, reproductive health and reproductive rights including contraceptive methods. The ICPD conference for the first time extended formal recognition a concern for adolescent reproductive and sexual health.

A review of health care system in India and the type of service provided clearly revealed that the Reproductive Health needs of Adolescents in India have 'largely been ignored'. The field of Adolescence Reproductive Health is still relatively new in the region. The health service in India have always been targeted more specifically to pregnant women, the infants and children and the nursing women, in fact, the adolescents who are prospective parents are glaringly neglected.

Adolescents are placed at continuing risk by their limited access to information on reproductive physiology, pregnancy and contraception, STDs and HIV/AIDS and other health related issues. It is essential that these adolescents are protected from unwanted sex, unwanted pregnancies, early child-bearing unsafe abortion, STDs and HIV/AIDS.

Education in general and Adolescence Reproductive Health Education in particular is being increasingly recognized as an important input for improving the health status of the population and also improving the quality of life of the individual. Adolescence is a receptive age when such and other value based life planning education can be imparted effectively. Thus, the early college years offer a good opportunity for imparting reproductive Health Education to the future parents. Imparting such education specially in view of existing social factors, however, remains a problem. Many studies have shown that in most instances Adolescents tend to learn about family life/reproductive health from unreliable source and in the process, pick up incorrect information. It is in this context that the need for educational response at the school and college about the various components of reproductive health education and enable the adolescents to cope with the problems of this transitional phase.

In the context of the present study, Adolescents developmental process, conception, pregnancy and child birth, contraceptives, STDs and HIV/AIDS were considered as the major components of the adolescence reproductive health education.

Many approaches have been used for imparting reproductive health education, the most common one being the face-to-face interaction. Because of social taboos attached to the subject its reach through face-to-face interaction is very limited. Against these constraints, distance education provides us with a cost effective and andragogically proven medium into the potential of a wide reach. The present research study describes the preliminary results of imparting reproductive health education through the distance mode using self-instructional materials. The study was designed to evaluate the effectiveness of self-instructional material on adolescence reproductive health education among the college adolescents.

The major objectives of the study are as under:

- To understand the level of knowledge and attitude among the college adolescents regarding adolescents reproductive health education at pre study and post study.
- To measure the effectiveness of self-instructional material on adolescence reproductive health education among the college adolescents in terms of knowledge gain and attitudinal change.
- To measure the difference in the effectiveness of self-instructional material on adolescents reproductive health education in terms of residence (Rural-Urban colleges); Sex (Male-Female); Course of study (Arts-Science); Age (17-18 years—19+ years) and school education (Urban-Rural school).

The specific objectives of the study are:

- To ascertain the effectiveness of the developed self-instructional material for college adolescents in terms of knowledge gain in the area of "Adolescents Development Process" through pre and post experimentation.
- To ascertain the effectiveness of the developed self-instructional material for college adolescents in terms of Attitude change in the area of "Adolescents developmental process" through pre and post experimentation.
- To ascertain the effectiveness of the developed self-instructional material for college adolescents in terms of knowledge gain in the area of "Family Life Education" through pre and post experimentation.

- To ascertain the effectiveness of the developed self-instructional material for college adolescents in terms of Attitude change in the area of "Family life education" through pre and post experimentation.
- To ascertain the effectiveness of the developed self-instructional material for college adolescents in terms of knowledge gain in the area of "Sexuality" through pre and post experimentation.
- To ascertain the effectiveness of the developed self-instructional material for college adolescents in terms of attitude change in the area of "Sexuality" through pre and post experimentation.
- To ascertain the effectiveness of the developed self-instructional material for college adolescents in terms of knowledge gain in the area of "STDs" through pre and post experimentation.
- To ascertain the effectiveness of the developed self-instructional material for college adolescents in terms of attitude change in the area of "STDs" through pre and post experimentation.
- To ascertain the effectiveness of the developed self-instructional material for college adolescents in terms of knowledge gain in the area of "HIV/AIDS" through pre and post experimentation.
- To ascertain the effectiveness of the developed self-instructional material for college adolescents in terms of attitude change in the area of "HIV/AIDS" through pre and post experimentation.

The study is limited only to the students of Under-Graduates in the selected colleges affiliated to University of Madras. The students chosen purposively for the study were only from the selected colleges.

2

Development and Family Life Education for Youth Global Studies

A Review

Literature is that mirror which reflects the past views and presents the future prospective. The previous literature gives guidelines and develops insight into the problems. So an essential aspect of an investigation in the reviews of related literature that is a general retrospective survey of previous writings pertaining to one's problem. In order to develop deep insight and to evaluate the methodological practices emerging out of researches, the researcher made a survey in the field of population education, adult education and adolescence education.

The literature on adolescent's reproductive health education in India is scanty. Not many comprehensive studies have been conducted on different dimensions of adolescence reproductive health education. However, elements of ARHE are found in several studies in India and abroad. An attempt was made in this chapter to review these studies with a view to assess their contribution and identify the gaps in the literature.

Studies from Developed and Developing Countries

CDC Study, U.S.A. (1994)

The CDC study sampled a cross-section of American Adolescents and sex education programmes throughout the United States. It urged further research and needs assessment studies that focus on changing attitudes, values beliefs and practices among the adolescent population.

The CDC study sampled a cross-section of American Adolescents and sex education programmes throughout the United States. It urged further research and needs assessment studies that focus on changing attitudes, values beliefs and practices among the adolescent population.

The CDC study establishes the point that the effectiveness of school based sex education programmes depends to a large extent on how they are linked to considerations that are at the heart of successful ARH interventions. The study cites clear linkages between these considerations and effective sex education programmes,

- Narrow focus on reducing sexual risk-taking behaviours that may lead to HIV/AIDS infection or unintended pregnancy.
- Application of social learning theories as a foundation for programme development.
- Provision of basic, accurate information about the risks of unprotected intercourse through experiential activities designed to personalize this information.
- Inclusion of activities that address social or media influences on sexual behaviours and the incidence of intercourse.
- Instruction about pregnancy and contraception positively influences the use of contraception at first intercourse and subsequent inter course.

WHO

WHO reviews 1050 scientific articles on sex education programmes and recommended the following;

- Sex education programmes should convey two types of messages for young people. One for those who have not begun sexual activities and another for those who are already sexually active.
- Sex education programmes should begin well before the age of 12 when young people start having sex and

- Sex education programmes should have as their goal the reduction of unplanned pregnancies as well the promotion of ways to reduce the incidence of unprotected intercourse. Teens that experience unprotected intercourse are vulnerable to STDs and unplanned pregnancies.

The review of a study coordinated by WHO working with UNFPA and UNICEF (1997) stresses the following needs,

- Identify and understand the target group
- Involve the youth in designing the programme
- Work with community leaders and parents to provide greater access to services.
- Incorporate evaluation in programme design, and
- Plan ways by which to sustain and expand successful services.

THE CASE STUDIES

Phillipines

In five large colleges and Universities in Manila, FAD recently conducted a campus based study on the sexual attitudes and behaviour of Filipino adolescents. The study revealed that a combination of societal familial, interpersonal and individual factors accounts for the growing number of young people who engage in pre-marital sex. Generally, partners engage in sexual intimacies depending on the length of their relationship in some cases, sexual contacts is triggered by a partner's financial need, use of drugs, search for physical pleasure (regardless of the presence or absence of love), membership in a fraternity or similar peer groups, and other related reasons.

Development and Family Life Education for Youth (DAFLEY)

The DAFLEY project is being carried out through the Davao teen center (DTC) which provides reproductive and sexual health care services through counseling, face to face or by telephone. Peer counseling, values formation and communication workshop preparing them emotionally, psychologically and even physically for the rigorous tasks ahead.

On the average the center receives 120 to 125 calls a month and up to 25 walks in youth, particularly on weekends. To accommodate youngsters who are to shy to come to the center, peer counselors arrange to meet them elsewhere. Counseling hours have been extended to 8.00 p.m.

Shine Project: Sexual Health Initiatives through Networking and Education. The project having made significant achievements in increasing the youths knowledge of important reproductive health issues and enabling them to make informed decisions about their reproductive life, it enables the youth to increase their knowledge and to focus on values that would guide them in making the right decisions about their reproductive life.

Magnolia

A KAP survey (1997) conducted by WHO among Mongolian adolescents showed that 78 per cent have inadequate health knowledge and that only 10 per cent observe healthy practices. Information on Reproductive Health and STD/AIDS is inadequate, with the youth depending mainly on radio and television. Youth people are reluctant to consult their parents and elders for fear of embarrassing them. Other preferred sources of information provided by friends are considered unreliable. The need to improve health educationalist the secondary school level and to incorporate it in the university curriculum is clearly felt.

Poor understanding of reproductive health and safe sex is particularly acute among young women and girls in the rural areas, giving rise to such misconceptions and abortion being the best protection and condom being a major cause of importance.

Nepal

The adolescents, especially those in the rural Nepal, have very little knowledge about sexual and reproductive health due to illiteracy and social taboos. The knowledge of puberty of menarche is virtually lacking among adolescent girl. They are unaware of the accompanying psychological changes that take place during and immediately after menarche. Moreover, they are often unable to discuss these issues with their parents due to social restrictions. These perception and misinformation often continue throughout their reproductive years.

A study on reproductive care knowledge, attitude and practices among adolescents sponsor by plan international in Makawanpur district found that there is a very high level of ignorance among adolescent girl about general hygiene or safe sanitation practices, during menstruation related health problems immediately before or at the end of their menstrual period and a large majority of girls experienced some symptoms of urinary tract infection (UTI).

Another study conducted by the valley Research group, Nepal revealed that there is a widespread lack of Knowledge about sexual acts among a substantial number of adolescents. More than 40 per cent of the adolescents admitted that they do not know anything about any type of sexual activities. About 72 per cent of male and 52 per cent of female adolescents acknowledge that they understand stage sex to some extent.

The center for Research on Environment Health and Population Activities (CREHPA) surveyed men in five border towns of Nepal. The survey showed that 41 per cent of unmarried adolescents of the 18-19 age group were sexually active. Among the sexually active unmarried men, 77 per cent had their first sexual intercourse while they were 19 years old. The same study showed that 10 per cent adolescent boys of the age group 15-19 were sexually active; 54 per cent of have multiple sex partners. About half of the sexually active adolescent boy did not believe that they were at risk of contracting STDs or HIV/AIDS only 27 per cent perceived the risk of contracting such diseases.

China

Studies done in Shanghai in 1995-1996 found that among the

2,580 respondents, 49.9 per cent did not know which part of the menstrual cycle were they vulnerable pregnancy. It seems that nobody, whether school teachers or employees, took the responsibility to show them the practical skills and methods of contraception.

Many KAP surveys administered in primary and secondary schools and college revealed that about 70 per cent of students know a little about human anatomy, about half of them were aware of ways of STI/HIV/AIDS transmission and non-transmission, but few 5 to 20 per cent depending on ages and areas were knowledgeable about pregnancy and contraception. Many studies indicated that about 70 per cent of teenagers received information about sex through magazines and mass media; 20 per cent from parents, friends and classmates; 4 per cent fro formal education in school and 6 per cent from other means, lacking proper channels of access for adolescents sex education, they some times turn to pornography or peers for sex information which is often misleading.

Studies done in colleges found that 15 to 25 percent of students respondents thought that sex is a matter of personal privacy and not the affair of society or community. Among the students, 5-10 percent of the females and 3-8 percent of females had already engaged in sex. Studies conducted in the cities of Beijing, Shanghai and others also revealed that 50-85 per cent of young women who appeared at premarital check-ups had sexual intercourse. Among them, 50-70 percent was below the age of 24.

Nearly half of the male college students and one-third of the female students had experienced masturbation. Many of them held the wrong notion that masturbation is seriously harmful to their health.

China

The adolescent reproductive health (ARH) pilot project was started in 1998 by the china family planning association under UNFPA project was undertaken in several high schools throughout Minghen district. Shanghai and in three universities in Beijing. They conducted a variety of interventions including peer education activities, lectures, quizzes, exhibitions, reading activities, development and distribution f IEC materials and leaflets computer education and a music concert. They used focus group discussions, interviews and self administered questionnaires for assessment. The results showed that many of the interventions were appropriate, systematic in design and relevant in content, thus having an effect on knowledge and attitude levels. Particularly, the peer education activities which were successful in providing the students with both knowledge and useful skills. The evaluation survey from shanghai showed that knowledge levels of students were raised at an average of 10 and 40 percent. Results from Beijing were harder to interpret as some of the knowledge levels dropped attitudes had not changed; they felt that the interventions helped them to clarify issues and become more secure in their opinions. In both Beijing and Shanghai, attitudes towards people living with AIDS become more positive.

Philippines

Young adult Fertility and Sexuality (YAFSS) of the university of Phiulippines presents some highlights. Of the country's total population of 70 million people, 49 per cent are below 20 years old. Of these, 20 per cent makeup 15-19 age group, 18 per cent or 2.5 million of those aged 15-24 had engaged in premarital sex. Among those who are 21 years old.

Premarital sex is not a one-time experience but is usually repeated. 70 per cent of the girls engage in repeated sex with the first partners, while 62 per cent of boys engage in repeated sex with at least another partner. The UNFPA funded Foundation for Adolescent Development (FAD) project is the mission to help young adults develop their potentials in becoming whole and emotionally secure through proper value formation, thereby making them self-reliant and productive individuals and responsible members of the community.

Bangladesh

Bashed, M.A. explains following: Typically, menarche occurs late due to poor nutritional habits. However, early marriage and pregnancy are common. Up to 15 per cent of births among teenage mothers occur before they have achieved full physical development, adversely affecting their general health, damaging their reproductive organs, and sometimes causing death-regarding less of their marital status, one if ten adolescent girls is a mother, compared with one in very four married, compared with one in every four married adolescent girls. It is estimated that 20 per cent of all rape victims are under the age of 16 adolescent accounts for 20 per cent of all sex workers.

Combodia

UNFPA supported survey on reproductive health among vulnerable youth found that contraceptive methods are very well known among the women and they had a good knowledge of various contraceptive methods including use of the pill, condoms and DPV.

The RHAC baseline study found that the knowledge of family planning was low given the sexual experience of the respondents. Less than a fifth (16% had heard of any method. Just over a third (33.6%) believed that sex before marriage would not result in pregnancy and 30.7 per cent of the respondents under 20 believed that sex before this age would result in pregnancy.

Many of the younger garment workers knew about contraception but their knowledge about reproductive physiology and fecundity was very poor only 18 per cent of garment workers were able to correctly identify the fertile period in the menstrual cycle. One third of young women said they could get pregnant the first time they had sexual intercourse, or if they had sex only once. A large proportion thought women were protected against pregnancy during their first encounter. Knowledge about conception was particularly poor among men, younger respondent and those with no schooling or incomplete primary schooling.

Two thirds of the respondents claimed they could not name any STD. A greater percentage from trait (80%) reported not to know many in the 11-15 age group, 73.8 per cent knew nothing about STDs compared to 55.9 per cent for the age group of 16.2 per cent a higher percentage of young women (71.6%) than young men (60.7%) had no knowledge at all about STDs. Actual knowledge of even one symptom was very limited. The most commonly known symptom was burning and itching and 5.4 per cent could identify this symptom. In relation to cures for STDs half of the respondents believed they could cure, less than a quarter stated they could not be cured and a similar number did not know.

They use of condoms to prevent STDs was mentioned by 90 per cent of the respondents who knew at least one STDs. Avoidance of sexual intercourse with commercial sex workers, monogamy and abstinence from sexual intercourse were also mentioned by one-third of the respondents as possible way to avoid STDs.

In the SCF survey on young people those who believed themselves not to be at risk of AIDS thought that they could still be possibly infected with AIDS anyway. One third of all respondents confirm this. To prevent the transmission of HIV/ AIDS 14.6 per cent thought that the best method would be to abstain from sex, a response to which more males in the 16-20 than the 11-15 age group agreed; and to which more males 21.5 per cent than female 9 per cent agreed.

The care survey of garment workers found that over 85 per cent of respondents had heard about HIV/AIDS (Sprechmann, 1997. A higher percentage of male than female workers and those with good literacy ski9lls had heard about the virus. The most influential source of information was mass media (95.37%) friends (39.8%) health workers (32.4%) posters/ leaflets (22.1%) relatives 19.5%) and teachers (8.5%).

They most risky form of transmission was recognized to be sexual intercourse with paid sex workers over two-third (67.7%) of young garment workers knew that HIV/AIDS could be transmitted through the sharing of needles and another 40 per cent through infected blood transfusion. Another 25 per cent noted that mothers could transmit the virus to their babies either prior to birth or through breast feeding.

Maldives

According to the reproductive health baseline survey conducted by the ministry of Health, Maldives knowledge of sexually transmitted disease is very low, about two thirds (65%) of the household respondents were unable to mention any symptom of STDs. However 99 per cent of the household respondents were aware of AIDS. There is a misconception that STDs can affect only a small proportion of population. On the other hand, data from 1995 revealed that 280 (24.7%) persons were sentenced for offences related to sexual activity outside of marriage. This figure included all age group however, the current trend indicates that the majority of sex offenders are adolescents.

LAO PDR

The central Lao youth union (LYU) is implementing the reproductive health programme which is supported by UNFPA and executed by JOICEP. A study was conducted on reproductive health among adolescents and young people between the ages of 15 and 24, the study covers their knowledge of birth spacing, contraceptives methods, their attitudes towards unwanted pregnancy, reproduction, STDs, HIV/AIDS and abuse and common youth practices concerning heterosexual relationship, discussions on se, planning for marriage and sex with commercial sex worker. The study covers 151 villages that have been randomly selected from one turn covers provinces.

Vietnam

The Vietnam government initiated the UNFPA funded project to promote adolescent reproductive health knowledge. An ARH mass media campaign implemented under the project focuses on promoting friendships, pure love and safe sexual behaviour and on increasing adolescent's access to reproductive health services. According to the survey report, only 53.8 per cent f the target group knew the terms "reproductive health" prior to the first campaign in '98, the figure rose to 95 per cent after the campaign. However there remains a great demand for reproductive health information among adolescents, an evaluation of the first campaign shoed that approximately 40 per cent of adolescent require more information. Another study recorded a higher figure of 78 per cent. Under this project, a national contest and the second campaign on reproductive health were organized.

Knowledge, Attitude and Behaviour on Sexuality and Reproductive Health

Very few unmarried youth aged 15-25 in rural areas had access to information sources. For instance, only 57.7 per cent of males and 48.9 per cent of females had heard of the term "Family Planning". For the youth the main sources of information on family planning were television (62.4%) and radio (50%) the young population of Vietnam is characterized by a low level of knowledge and understanding of sexual, family planning and use of contraceptives they know little or nothing about sexuality, contraception and contraceptive methods safe sex and how to negotiate safe sex (population council et al.97) A survey of 1464 unmarried students showed that only 42 per cent of then gave a correct answer about the most fertile time in a woman's menstruation cycle. A survey in a city also showed that nearly a third of 15-19 years old students did not know the fertile period of women.

A study done by the youth union among young, unmarried women who had obtained abortion services in Hanoi, Hai Hung province proved that the major reason for unwanted pregnancies was the youth's ignorance of sexuality, sex and reproductive health. In the meantime only 70 per cent of females and 56.3 per cent percent of males of this age group were aware of the potential consequences of abortion. The youth awareness of STDs was also limited with the exemption of HIV/AIDS. Only a quarter of them were aware of syphilis and even fewer 23.6 per cent had ever heard of gonorrhea. Studies had shown that as many as 96-98 per cent of the urban and or college youth heard about HIV/AIDS and a large proportion of them also knew its source of transmission (NAAC, 1997; Good kind and A.H. 1997; Lan and Hoa, 1996)

A survey of 4446 adolescents aged 10-19 in Hanoi, Vinh and Thai Binh showed that most of them (98.3%) could name HIV/AIDS as sexually transmitted diseases but very few could spontaneously list other STDs. Only 32.2 per cent of them could name gonorrhea and 29.7 per cent could name syphilis. The other STDs such as chlamydiosis and herpes were listed by less than 1 per cent of the respondents. When asked about the prevention of these disease, three quarters of them mentioned condom, 55.7 per cent mentioned having only one sexual partner and 32.1 per cent said avoidance of drugs.

Qualitative studies revealed that sexual relations were considered by many as a natural part of romantic relationships. With respect to premarital sex, between 41.1 per cent and 79.3 per cent would approve this is difference contexts such as an agreement between both partners (44.8%) with much love (51%) with an intention of marriage (79.3%) and as an expression of love (41.1%) (Nga and Hong, 1997). The percentage of the unmarried youth involved in sexual activities varies from 0.7 per cent to 72 per cent depending on study sites (rural, urban) and age group of respondents.

Agampodi, S.B.; Agampodi, T.C.; UKD, P. (2008) studied adolescents perception of reproductive health care services in Sri Lanka. The purpose of this study was to explore the perceived reproductive health problems, health seeking behaviours, knowledge about available services and barriers to reach services among a group of adolescents in Sri Lanka in order to improve reproductive health service delivery. This qualitative study was conducted in a semi urban setting in Sri Lanka. A convenient sample of 32 adolescents between 17-19 years of age participated in four focus group discussions.

Participants were selected from four midwife areas. A pre-tested focus group guide was used for data collection. Male and female facilitators conducted discussions separately with young males and females. All tape-recorded data was fully transcribed and thematic analysis was done. Psychological distresses due to various reasons and problems regarding menstrual cycle and masturbation were reported as the commonest health problems. Knowledge on existing services was very poor and boys were totally unaware of youth health services available through the public health system. On reproductive Health Matters, girls mainly sought help from friends whereas boys did not want to discuss their problems with anyone. Lack of availability of services was pointed out as the most important barrier in reaching the adolescent needs. Lack of access to reproductive health knowledge was an important reason for poor self-confidence among adolescents to discuss these matters. Lack of confidentiality, youth friendliness and accessibility of available services were other barriers discussed. Adolescents were happy to accept available services through public clinics and other health infrastructure for their services rather than other organizations. A demand was made for separate youth friendly services through medical practitioners. Adolescent health services are inadequate and available services are not being delivered in an acceptable manner. Proper training of health care providers on youth friendly service provision is essential. A National level integrated health care programme is needed for the adolescents.

Mngadi P.T., Faxelid E., Zwane I.T., Höjer B. & Ransjo-Arvidson A.-B. (2008) studied Health providers' perceptions of adolescent sexual and reproductive health care in Swaziland. The study was carried out among fifty-six healthcare providers, working in 11 health clinics in Swaziland in 2005, using a semi-structured questionnaire. The data were analysed by descriptive statistics and content analysis to identify key themes. Most participants were women with a mean age of 36 years and a mean number of 6 years in the profession. Services provided included STIs/HIV/AIDS advice, pre- and post-test counseling and testing on HIV, contraceptives and condom use. Half of the nurses/midwives had no continued education and lacked supervision on adolescent sexual and reproductive health care. The majority had unresolved moral doubts, negative attitudes, values and ethical dilemmas towards abortion care between the law, which is against abortion, and the reality of the adolescents' situation. Forty-four wanted to be trained on post-abortion care while eight on how to perform abortions. Twenty-six wanted the government to support adolescent-friendly services and to train healthcare providers in adolescent sexual and reproductive health services.

Conclusion

The study findings concludes that curricula within nursing and midwifery preservice education need to be reviewed to incorporate comprehensive services for adolescents. There is need for provision of comprehensive services for adolescents in Swaziland and appropriate youth-friendly services at all levels. There is need for nurse/midwifery participation, advocacy and leadership in policy development.

Uddin J., Choudhury A.M. (2008) studied Reproductive health awareness among adolescent girls in rural Bangladesh. The study revealed that a sizable proportion of adolescent girls had incorrect knowledge or misconceptions about the fertile period, reproduction, sexually transmitted diseases, and HIV/AIDS. Age, education either of adolescents or their mothers, residence, and exposure to mass media were the significant predictors of adolescent girls' knowledge about reproductive health. Strong efforts are needed to improve awareness and to clarify misconceptions about reproductive health. Improved access to mass media and education could improve rural Bangladesh Adolescent girls' awareness about reproductive health.

Studies Conducted in India

According to the national family health survey (1992) the

knowledge of HIV/AIDS and STDs is very low among girls in the age group of 13-19. Most adolescents tend to be extremely unaware of their own bodies, their health, physical well-being and sexually this is particularly true among the younger adolescents. Attitude towards marriage and sex among adolescents in India continue to be conservative and accepting of traditional norms that oppose marriage with self-selected partners, social interaction between adolescent boys and girls and premarital sexual activities among Indian adolescents. Yet, it has been observed that knowledge regarding reproductive health among them is limited. They have very little accurate information on the process of growing up and on pre-marital, marital and extra-marital sexual relationship.

IEC Strategies: Telephone Counseling

Telephone counseling services have been envisaged a one of the significant components of the third phase of the population and development education the higher education project. Telephone and personal counseling are significant and effective means of communication for adolescents. Counseling services were therefore and available at all Population Education Resource Centre (PERC). The four major areas, considered, as thrusts for adolescents are Adolescent Sexuality, HIV/AIDS drug abuse and Care-related questions. Services are given free, confidential and done by experts trained medical officers or peer educators. The telephone counseling approach has been found correct information and guidance to students.

Ramanathan, et al., (2000) Center for Development Studies conducted a study in Kerala from two districts, one the best performing and the other, one of the not so good performing districts, were selected for analysis. The analysis revealed that there is a need to improve quality of services in terms of training gross root level workers to provide better information to clients and to supply them with better equipment. This would empower clients of the RCS Programme in Kerala to make well informed contraceptive choices.

Ram, Usha (2000) PRC, Pune conducted a survey-I two

tribal community development blocks of the Thane district of Maharastra. The survey was conducted from 1295 women from 16 villages, out of the total 2169 pregnancies/deliveries recorded during the reference period, about 74 per cent were wanted whereas the remaining 26 per cent were either mistimed or were never wanted. Further, among those reported unwanted, nearly 16 per cent were is mistimed while remaining 10 per cent were not wanted at all.

Susuman, Sathya (1997) conducted a study to find out the relationship between sex preference of children and contraceptive practice among the tribal communities in the Nilgiris district of Tamilnadu. The analysis mainly focused on measurement of sex preference, and its influence upon contraceptive practice and fertility, as tribal population is still not fully explored in the case of their sex preference attitude and contraceptive practice was directed to these groups. The non-tribal groups, who are also inhabitants of the nearby areas of the tribal settlements, have been also given similar attention in this study with regard to the issue discussed the study of accurate comparison. The result reveal that fertility pattern among tribes are quite different from the rest of the population, the sex preference is strong the tribal couple with three of more children.

Anil Kumar (2000) analyses the pattern of pregnancy risk in the major states of India. Also it analyses the structural determinants of pregnancy risk in India. The analysis revealed the fact that female adult literacy plays an important role in reducing the risk of pregnancy. Another note worthy feature of the analysis is that pregnancy risk lesser impact on infant mortality. This implies that there are more important factors apart from these risks, which result in high infant mortality. The analysis suggested the need for increasing the knowledge about reproductive health among women especially the illiterates.

From a multivariate analysis study, Sayeed Unisa (1999) concluded that the son's preference exists irrespective of women's education and other socio-economic characteristic.

Traditional Indian society needs at least one son for the family. The magnitude of preference for son among northern belt is many times more than southern states. Many women in northern states are not stopping child bearing till they get at least one son this may be one of the important determinants for high fertility in north India. It is quite surprising that women with one son going for nest child is not desiring daughter as next child, this clearly shows that in north India preference for son exists strongly. Along with this avoidance for girl child is also prevailing.

As a part of Reproductive and Child Health Programme, IIPE, Mumbai (Ram, F., Sanjay, M., 1998) conducted rapid household survey which has been carried out in 252 districts in India to provide monitoring indicators on various RCH programme at district level. The results showed that 37 of the 245 district have low CBR (less than 20) whereas in 79 districts it high (greater than 30). There are 61 districts in which current use of family planning is low (less than 30%) as compared to 60 districts with more has 60 per cent of current use. The coverage of complete immunization showed that, in 150 districts complete immunization is less than 50 per cent as compared to more than 75 per cent in 71 districts. The cross classification of CBR, family planning uses and services coverage with respect to mother's education has shown substantial variation. The correlation coefficient of mother's education with respect to birth rate, current use of family planning, unmet need for family planning and service coverage is found to be strong and significant. Similarly the correlation coefficient of child survival, safe motherhood and family planning use has shown strong and significant association.

Goyal and Rahul (2000) studied the perspectives attitude and behaviour of men and women towards sexual health, assess their information needs in the context and to carryout a health education and health promotion programme to meet these needs. The study was conducted in selected rural and urban localities of Ajmer and Udaipur districts of Rajasthan during 1997-1999 covering 2000 married men and women in sexuality active age group. A series of qualitative data showed that there was a large gap in men and women understands of sexual health. Also there was a poor appreciation for women's sexuality both by men and women. Sixteen percent men have admitted that they have extramarital sexual relationship. However, only 25 of them were using condom as a protection against STD/HIV the level of awareness for STDs was large but very few men and women knew about HIV/AIDS.

Tiwari, V.K. and Anil Kumar (2000) conducted a study on premarital sex and unmet need of contraception among unmarried youth in slums of Delhi and Lucknow. The study data was collected from 254 youths in Delhi and 212 youths from Lucknow. Youths were randomly selected from 5 slums in Delhi and 3 slums in Lucknow information on their socio-demographic background, family environment employment, income and expenditure pattern, behaviour, knowledge about certain reproductive facts and safe sex, myths, experiencing pre-marital sex and need of contraceptives were collected through pre-tested semi-structural questionnaire. The findings reveal that large percentage of youths frequently seeing blue films and porno-literature, partially employed having poor knowledge of contraceptive and safe sex (50%) indulged in unsafe sex practice (30%) with more than one partner. The need of sex education through mass media and availability of condoms within slums were found the study.

Suresh Kumar (2000) analysed the knowledge of AIDS and the attitude towards people with Aids among the male and female workers in the unorganized sector in Thiruvananthapuram City, Kerala. The analysis shows that the level of AIDS knowledge of the respondents especially that of women is very poor. Only half of the male and about quarters of the female workers have adequate knowledge of HIV/AIDS. These points towards the immediate need to strengthen the existing programmes on HIV/AIDS. The change for attaining HIV/AIDS knowledge is found to vary significantly with education and income in the case of male respondents and with level of income and area of residence in the case of female respondents, in the multivariate analysis. It is shocking to see that rise in AIDS knowledge leads to a negative attitude towards people with AIDS, among male respondents. It reveals the inefficiency of the existing AIDS awareness programme to develop a positive attitude towards people with AIDS.

Shirur, R. Rajani, Kapali & Nagarajan (1996) carried at a study in the selected colleges of Madras City wherein HIV/ AIDS awareness campaign were organized in their colleges and also in their respective communities adopted by them. The study findings are;

- Male students possess slightly higher level of awareness on AIDS as compared to female students.
- However it is interesting to find that participation in AIDS awareness campaign has not specially made any difference because a higher percentage of non-participants appear to possess higher level of awareness.
- With regard to awareness of students belonging to different causes of study, commerce students appear to have performed much better followed by Science and Arts students.
- There is no difference in the attitude of students between sexes, by participation or by courses.
- The awareness of students on high risk factors by sex and by participation obviously, no difference is observed between the sexes or with the participation or non-participation of students.

Nagarajan, Kapali and Shirur (1998) conducted a survey under the UGC project among the college students of Madras University. The findings reveal that;

- Female students are more aware than the male students with regard to population and demography.
- There is no significant difference between male and female students with regard to AIDS awareness.
- More number of Arts and Science students were more aware than the commerce students regarding HIV/ AIDS.

- More number of female students was better aware of Health aspects.
- Majority of students, both male and female students were having inadequate level of awareness about the drug abuse and alcohol.
- Generally, majority of students were having higher level knowledge regarding HIV/AIDS.

The Thoughtshop Foundation (1999) conducted a study of the sexual health problems and information need of young people in urban and rural West Bengal. The study findings point to an almost total lack of awareness of sexual health issues and knowledge of the Human anatomy among the target population and the people who influence them most parents and teachers. Very often the very same people discourage young people's access to information about sexual health.

A study on knowledge, attitude, beliefs and practices among urban educated Indian Youth (1993-94) conducted by the Family Planning Association of India and 15 centers of the Sex Education Counseling Research and Training Therapy (SECRT) department offer interesting findings; It observed that the Indian youth lack access to sources of correct information on sexual/health matters, with many relying on the mass media and peer groups. The study further noted that more males than females have correct sexual/health knowledge on the average, males have their first sexual experience at age 16, and females at 18. The study urged the introduction of sex education in the schools and the provision of appropriate training to teachers. The goal is to ensure that the Indian youth is able to cope with the changing physical, biological, and emotional needs of growing up from adolescence of adulthood.

Madan Singh, et al., (2000) State Resource Centre studied knowledge, attitude and behaviour of Adolescent learners regarding gender equality, small family norms, reproductive health and reproductive rights in the district of Raebareli, U.P. The major findings of the study were;

- The majority of learners had the knowledge of small

family norms but there were about 25.6 per cent learners belonging to rural areas and 26.0 per cent of urban learners did not get the idea of two children norm.

- The son preference was shown by majority of learners belonging to scheduled caste (95.6%) followed by OBCs (92.5%) minorities (85%) and others (75%).
- The majority of Adolescent females of urban area had heard the family planning (63.6%) while the percentage of such learners of rural area (42.3%) was comparatively low.
- It was found that right of intercourse was mainly with the husband and therefore there were chances of spreading the disease to the husbands whose wives were infected with STDs.
- The study indicated that majority of learners did not know that infertility may occur in females. Infertility as a disease was not known to majority of learners, only 39.9 per cent learners were aware that infertility in women was a disease. Only a few of adolescents were aware that it is also curable.

Pai, S.C. (1981) studied on preparation and try out of curriculum in environmental studies leading to life-long education for college students. The main findings of the study were;

- There was significant difference in the performance of the experimental group as compared to control group on knowledge score and attitude score.
- The experimental group had gained more than the control group in environmental activities inventory indicating effectiveness of the curriculum.
- Unit-wise analysis of the performance of the students in the experimental group showed that they have gained over all knowledge in environmental problems as a result of the knowledge gained from the new curriculum.

Jurial, G.S. (1981) prepared instructional materials for developing creativity in students and assessed the effectiveness of verbal and non-verbal instructional materials in the development of creativity of students. It was found that;

- The post test creativity mean scores of students of verbal and non-verbal experimental groups were significantly higher than those of the students of the verbal and non-verbal control groups.
- Adolescents represent almost one quarter of the population in India and that adolescents are rarely considered a distinct group with special needs apart from those of children and adults. Moreover, much of the available information is recent and exploratory.
- While adolescent sexual behaviour, sexual awareness, and attitudes remain poorly explored topics, and available findings are not entirely representative. Regarding sexual activity, the available evidence suggests that between 20-30 percent of all males and upto 10 per cent of all females are sexually active during adolescence before marriage. Sexual awareness seems to be largely superficial.
- Awareness of STDs and AIDS is particularly limited among all groups, young and poorly educated adolescents in urban slums. Even among urban college students AIDS awareness is not universal. It is particularly poor among low-income slum adolescents. Far worse, knowledge about HIV/AIDS its modes of transmission and the role of condom in safe sex were poorly understood by all, irrespective of age and educational status.
- Contraceptive awareness is equally vague, even among married adolescents. Accurate knowledge of method is even more limited. Knowledge of sex and reproductive are even more limited among adolescent, whether educated or not. Adolescents tend to be extremely poorly informed regarding their own sexuality and physical well being their health, and their

bodies. Whatever knowledge they have, more over, is incomplete and confused.

After reviewing of related literature it is concluded that several efforts on curriculum development, Instructional materials preparations and self learning have been made in foreign countries as well as in Indian situation concerned. The findings of these researchers were helpful to mould the curriculum according to existing needs of the adolescent learners. These studies shows the weaknesses of curriculum at different levels and also helped to suggest the novel ideas related to learning experiences, content and instructional strategies. The studies on adolescent's reproductive health education revealed that awareness in the learners towards their scientific, social and cultural environment is a significant approach.

Thus it can be said whatever researches conducted in the field of population education have no relevance with the prevailing conditions and far from realistic situation, which create dilemma of mental exercises. Here the investigator has tried to synthesize the nature of the content according to the urgent need of the adolescent learners in their own environment. This has to enhance the efficacy of the content provided to them as well as sustain their inner urge to read and motivate for desirable learning.

3

Adolescents Reproductive Health Education

Research Methodology

This chapter deals with the methodology of the study, the research design, population/sample, experimental manipulation used in the research (measurement process, content selection and preparation) stages of experimental study, study tools construction, data collection, data analysis and other aspects related to the experimental research.

Design and Procedure of the Study

The procedure, an important phase of research and the design of the study, is of prime importance in attracting research problem in a scientific manner. Kerlinger (1973) defined research design as "the plan, structure and strategy of investigation conceived so as to obtain answers to research questions and control variance" The plan includes an outline of what the investigator will do from writing the hypothesis to the final analysis of the operation of variables. The strategy implies how the research objectives will be researched.

Empirical researches in social sciences are conducted in a variety of settings and contexts where the choice of research method is depending upon the nature of questions being asked, the types of answers sought and the degree of experimental control desired. In this study, the learning is knowledge gain and attitude change, is the focal point in the process of adolescents reproductive health development through self-instructional/learning modules in the quasi-experimental approach.

Quasi Experimental Design

The phrase "quasi experimental design" refers to the applications of or experimental mode of analysis and interpretation to bodies of data not meeting the full requirements of experimental control. The circumstances in which it is appropriate are those of experimentation in social settings including planned interventions where complete experimental control may not be possible. Quasi experiments correspond to certain natural settings, in which the experiment can approximate experimental procedures for collecting data, even though the researcher lacks full control over the delivery of treatment (Stempel & Bruce, 1981).

The original design conceived of the on-going developmental programmes/reproductive Health programmes on our control/pre-study and the treatment of giving the developmental/Reproductive Health Education as additional inputs for change over and above the developmental programmes. Hence the change that occurred in the pre-study/control must be subtracted from the post study in the treatment in order to assess the net impact of the treatments.

The design of the research project is set under the following heads.

Phase One

A. Design and Development of Self-Instructional Materials

1. Selection of research areas for the proposed self-instructional: The investigator selected 7 components of Adolescents Reproductive Health Education for the preparation of self-instructional materials for the college adolescents.
2. Selection of contents: The term content includes facts, concepts, definition and principles. The content of the curriculum should include those items which are helpful to achieve the educational objectives of the curriculum. In order to fulfill the objectives of the study, content for the research area's Adolescents

Reproductive Health Education was selected. First of all suitable/relevant components under major content area of ARHE were arranged in units. Under these six units all the 12 topics were grouped. For every units/ topics were designed with relevant illustration and an evaluation question with answer keys.

The lessons that comprise the curriculum were derived from various manuals, hand books, teachers guides, source books and other forms of curriculum materials and reports tat have been prepared in developing countries for use in their respective adolescents Reproductive Health Education programmes. Most of these lessons have been adopted to approximate their suitability to the Indian situation. The following publications have been served as primary sources for this self-learning package;

- Adolescence Education, UNESCO, Principal Regional Office for Asia and the Pacific, Bangkok, 1991.
- School Health Education to prevent AIDS and sexually transmitted diseases.
- A resource package for curriculum planners, WHO/ UNESCO. 1990.
- Handbook for Educating on Adolescent Reproductive and Sexual Health UNESCO/PROAP, Regional clearing House on population Education and Communication/ UNFPA. Bangkok, 1998.
- Education in Human Sexuality, FPAI, 1998.

The prepared material was field tested and found to be beneficial to the college Adolescents.

B. Selection and preparation of Contents/Learning Modules

Based on the pre-survey, the investigator selected the following five broad areas related to Reproductive Health Education of College Adolescents.

1. Physical, emotional and psychological changes during adolescence

2. Human Reproductive system/function/sexuality
3. Conception, pregnancy, Child birth and contraceptives.
4. Abortion, Pre-marital sex and Adolescence pregnancy-ill effects.
5. Sexually Transmitted Diseases (STDs) and HIV/AIDS.

After discussion with the experts and taking into consideration of logistics, the contents/units under each broad areas of Adolescents Reproductive Health Education were finalized. The details are given below;

(a) Physical changes during adolescence period
(b) Emotional/psychological changes
(c) Reproductive systems and functions, male and female
(d) Marriage, Legal age at marriage
(e) Conception, pregnancy and child-birth
(f) Contraceptive methods
(g) Abortion, illegal abortion and its consequences.
(h) Adolescence pregnancy- its ill effects
(i) Pre-marital sex-its consequences
(j) Sexually Transmitted Diseases (STDs)
(k) HIV/AIDS

Phase Two

It involved;
(a) Construction of study tools
(b) Sampling procedures
(c) Data collection

(a) Construction of Study Tools

Taking into consideration of the variables, characteristics of the selected samples and the nature of research design, the investigator has developed the following tools; a. Knowledge b. Attitude

The knowledge and attitude schedule consisted of 80 questions meant for assessing the knowledge attitude and behaviour of the students at pre-survey of the experiment. The given table will provide the details of the question framed for measuring the level of knowledge, attitude and behaviour of the college adolescents of the Reproductive Health education components.

S. No.	*Reproductive Health Education Units*	*Knowledge No. of questions*	*Attitude No. of questions*
1.	Personal information 5 items		
2.	Physical changes during adolescence	1(10)	3
3.	Psychological changes	1(8)	—
4.	Marriage, Age at Marriage	7	—
5.	Conception, pregnancy and child birth	6(16)	10
6.	Contraceptive methods	2(5)	—
7.	Abortions, adolescence pregnancy	6(5)	—
8.	Sexually Transmitted Diseases (STDs)	5(14)	5
9.	HIV/AIDS	6(22)	7

Apart from the above dimensions, 4 (9) items /questions for assessing the menstrual problems of the girl students and one (8) question for assessing the attitude towards opposite sex and also asked about their premarital sexual behaviour were added with the questionnaire. The questionnaire was checked for content validity and relevance to the questions by three experts in the subjects. The prepared questionnaire was pre-tested in a college with the Home Science students for uniform understanding of the statements. Based on the response certain questions were rewritten in more simple language, few items were repeated and also certain unwanted questions were deleted. The revised questionnaire was again tested and found to meet the researcher's requirements. The finalized questionnaire is containing 78 items which included a knowledge inventory and a Likert type response scale to assess the respondent's attitude in the subjects mentioned in the table.

(b) Sampling Procedures

The study sample comprised 509 students I year Under Graduate classes from 10 colleges, 6 colleges from Chennai City and 4 College from rural colleges, affiliated to Madras University Tamilnadu. The initial contact was the principal of the college, who sent a memorandum, information to all his/ her faculty members introducing the Investigator and the Research Project, and requesting their participation. The investigator then, individually contacted the faculties of Arts and Sciences and requested their permission to conduct the survey among the students in their classes. In given department, one in Arts and another in Science, only those faculty members who were easily available and who taught the required courses were contacted.

The rational for the choice of the required courses was that these courses would increase the possibility of contacting almost all the students within a class contact with the students

Sample Distribution

S. No.	*Colleges*	*Arts*			*Science*			*Total*		
		M	*F*	*T*	*M*	*F*	*T*	*M*	*F*	*T*
A. Urban Colleges										
1.	Govt. Arts College Chennai-35	35	—	35	19	—	19	54	—	54
2.	The New College, Chennai-14	12	—	12	29	—	29	41	—	41
3.	Gurunanak College, Chennai	13	15	28	13	15	28	26	30	56
4.	Bharathi College for Women, Chennai	—	23	23	—	31	31	—	54	54
5.	Quaid-e-Millet Govt. College, Chennai	—	25	25	—	18	18	—	43	43
6.	Women's Christian College, Chennai-6	—	13	13	—	47	47	—	60	60
B. Rural Colleges										
1.	Pachayappa's College (Men), Kancheepuram	20	—	20	40	—	40	60	—	60
2.	Pachayappa's College (w omen), Kancheepuram	—	21	21	—	26	26	—	47	47
3.	Auxilium College, Vellore	—	25	25	—	26	26	—	51	51
4.	Muthurangam Govt. College, Vellore	—	22	22	—	21	21	—	43	43
	Total	**80**	**144**	**224**	**101**	**184**	**285**	**181**	**328**	**509**

were made and the survey conducted during the scheduled class period. Total of 550 questionnaires were distributed, completed and collected during the pre-study. Of these 41 questionnaires were removed from the sample as they were; Uncompleted (32) Age above 20 years (9). Of the remaining sample of 509 were taken into consideration for the final analysis.

(c) Data Collection

Recognizing that it was a sample of convenience, an attempt was made to contact instructors/faculties from different disciplines so as to obtain a sample that could provide both variability and typically in the students' attitudes and behaviours. Given the sensitive nature of few items it was considered important to spend at least 15 minutes prior to the survey to build a rapport and create an atmosphere of trust and to provide assurance of anonymity. The students were instructed need not write their name and to deposit their answered questionnaires in a box on the table, similar procedures were followed at all the selected colleges.

The investigator has briefed the students initially the objectives of the projects and their responsibility in the project. Then the pre structured self administered anonymous questionnaires were distributed to them. They were asked to work independently in the presence of the investigator. The students of I year in Arts subject and science subjects, in each college one class of Arts subject and one class of science subject were taken as the sample from that college. Soon after the pre survey, the self-instructional materials were distributed to the students along with feedback forms. Three weeks time was given to them for reading the given materials. Then the feedback forms were collected from the students. After a week time the post survey was conducted. The questionnaire, which was used in the pre survey, was used in the post survey also. The learners, who dropped out in between the pre survey and post survey were not studied.

Analysis

The respondent's degree of reproductive health Knowledge was assessed by a 30 item inventory. The item deals with adolescent's physical, psychological changes, marriage, conception, pregnancy, childbirth, contraceptives, sexuality, premarital sex, abortion and STD, HIV/AIDS. Each knowledge question was answered as either "Yes", "No" or "Don't know". The responses don't know option was provided to reduce the guessing factor and was treated as on incorrect answer. The score on the knowledge was obtained by adding the number of correct answer that the respondents gave. The respondent's attitude towards reproductive Health Education components was assessed by a total of 26 items of Likert type response scale is Agree, Disagree and undecided. Score on the attitude sub-scales were obtained for each respondent by assigning a value of " through " for response options ranging from agree (3) to Disagree (1) with an uncertain midpoint (2) (including reverting negative items) and obtaining the mean score for each area.

Operational Definitions

Adolescents: The first year Under Graduate students in the age group of 17-19 years were considered as the target group. The students who were not married were included in the study.

Knowledge: Knowledge is a body of understood information possessed by an individual or by a culture. It is also that part of a person's information which is in accordance with established fact (English and English, 1958)

Attitude: Allport (1935) defines attitude as a mental and neural state of readiness, exerting a directive influence upon the individual's response to all subjects and situations with which it is related. According to Sills (1968) 'An attitude is a relatively enduring organization of beliefs around an object or situation predisposing one to respond in some preferential manner'.

Self-Instructional Materials: The term self-instructional materials mean to develop literature in a series of simple steps designed to lead the learners from which they will read and understand independently. All these self-instructional materials which enable the learners to keep up, use and develop knowledge, they have acquired and the abilities generated through self-learning.

The subsequent chapter deals with the analysis and interpretation of data.

4

The Data Speak

Analysis and Interpretation

In this chapter the Investigator analysed the data of the present study objectives wise with their corresponding null hypotheses. For developing this chapter each objective of the present study has been stated. The researcher divided the whole research area into five different units. For testing each objective, researcher formulated five corresponding null hypotheses-relating to each unit. The whole analysis of the present study is as follows;

4.1. Profile of the Students

The profile of the sampled students is given in the following tables. The total sample is consisted of 509 college students.

Table 4.1: Distribution of College Students by Sex

Sl. No	*Sex*	*Frequency*	*Percentage*
1.	Male	224	44
2.	Female	285	56
	Total	**509**	**100**

Considering the sex of the students the sample consisted of 224 (44%) male and 285 (56%) female students.

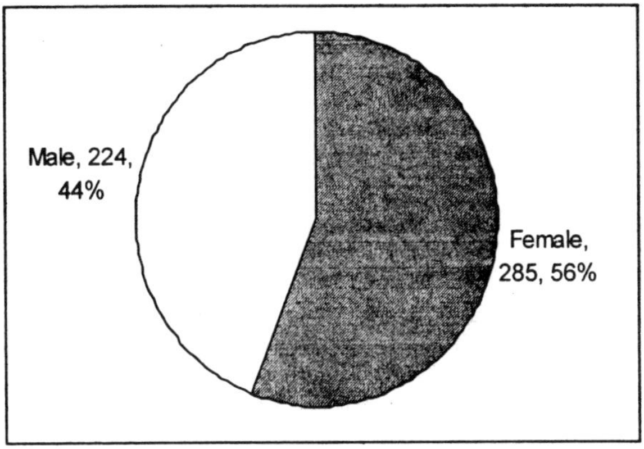

Fig. 4.1: Distribution of College Students by Sex

Table 4.2: Distribution of College Students by Education Stream

Sl. No.	*Education Stream*	*Frequency*	*Percentage*
1.	Arts	223	44
2.	Science	286	56
	Total	**509**	**100**

The above table indicates that majority of students (56%) are studying Science subjects and only 44 per cent are studying Arts subjects.

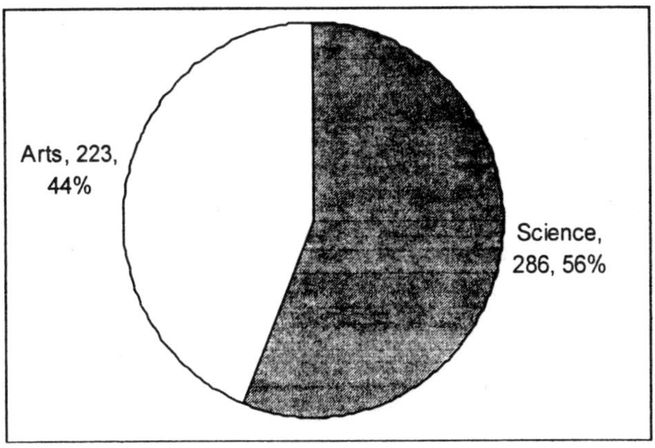

Fig. 4.2: Distribution of Students by Education Stream

Table 4.3: Distribution of College Students by Rural and Urban college

Sl. No.	*College*	*Frequency*	*Percentage*
1.	Rural college	201	39
2.	Urban college	308	61
	Total	**509**	**100**

The analysis of the study on distribution of students by Rural and Urban colleges are indicated that majority of the students belongs to Urban colleges (61%) followed by Rural colleges (39%).

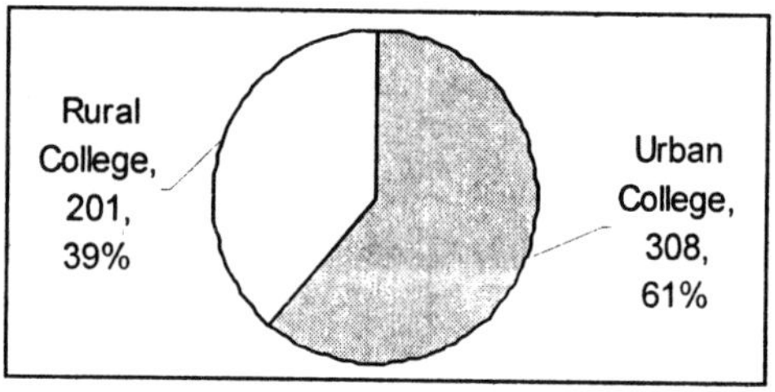

Fig. 4.3: Distribution of Students by Rural and Urban college

Table 4.4: Distribution of Students by School Education

S. No.	*School*	*Frequency*	*Percentage*
1.	Urban School	334	66
2.	Rural School	175	34
	Total	**509**	**100**

Table 4.4. Indicates that majority of students (66%) studied in urban schools and only 34 per cent of students studied in rural schools.

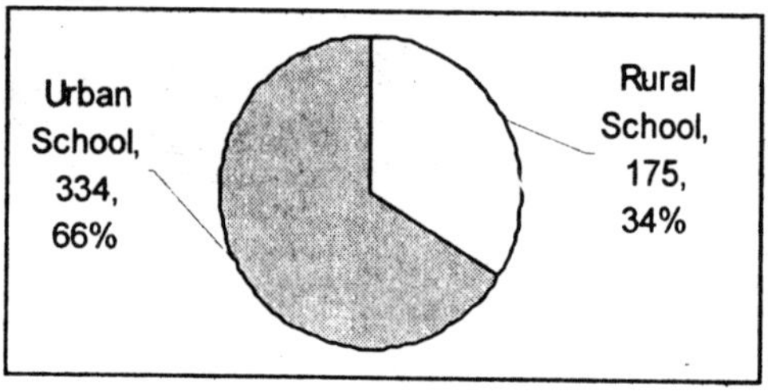

Fig. 4.4: Distribution of Students by School Education

Table 4.5: Distribution of College Students by Age

Sl. No.	*Age*	*Frequency*	*Percentage*
1.	17-18 years	288	57
2.	19+ years	221	43
	Total	**509**	**100.**

The table indicates 57 per cent of students belong to 17-18 years age group and only 43 per cent belong to 19+ year age group.

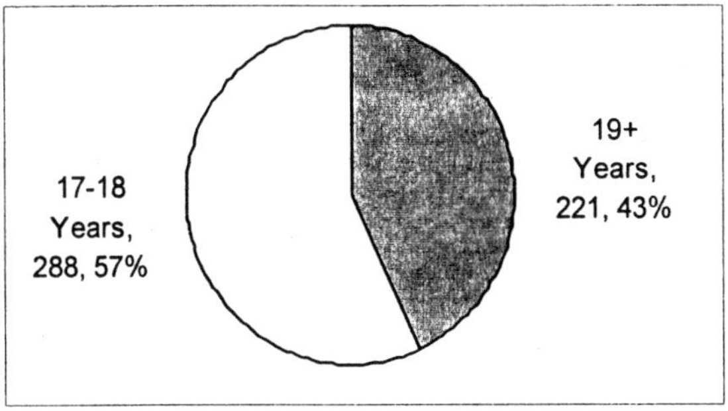

Fig. 4.5: Distribution of College students by Age

I

ADOLESCENCE DEVELOPMENT PROCESS

Knowledge

Objective

To ascertain the effectiveness of the developed self-instructional material for college adolescents in terms of knowledge gain in the area of 'Adolescence Development Process' through pre and post experimentation. The Investigator formulated five corresponding Null-Hypotheses of this objective, which are as follows.

Hypothesis No.: 1.1.0: There will be no significant difference between the achievement (knowledge Gain) of Rural College students and Urban college students through learning of Self-Instructional material on "Adolescence Development Process".

Table 1.1.0: Mean scores of students knowledge before and after studying self instructional material on "Adolescence Development Process" by Rural and Urban Colleges

	Rural College			*Urban college*			*'t' value*
	N	*Mean*	*SD*	*N*	*Mean*	*SD*	
Pre study	201	15.55	3.79	308	16.091	3.22	1.1978
Post study	201	16.861	3.14	308	17.182	3.06	0.8109
	't' value=2.682			**'t' value=3.048**			

The mean scores obtained at the pre study and post study were presented in Table No. 1.1.0. The data in table indicated that both the Rural College students and urban college students did not differ significantly in their knowledge level in the area of 'Adolescence Development Process' at the pre study. In other word they were comparable in terms of their level of knowledge on 'Adolescence Development Process'.

After learning the self-instructional materials on 'Adolescence Development Process' both Rural college students and Urban college students groups changed very significantly in their knowledge level on "Adolescence Development Process". The result indicated that there was significant learning taking place through self-instructional material on "Adolescence Development Process" among the students of these two groups.

But whereas when comparing the mean scores of knowledge at post study these two groups were not significant. It indicated that the learning among these two groups of students was taking place uniformly.

Hypothesis No. 1.2.0: There will be no significant difference between the achievement (knowledge gain) of Male and Female students through learning of self-instructional material on "Adolescence Development Process".

Table 1.2.0: Mean scores of students Knowledge before and after studying self-instructional material on "Adolescence Development Process" by Sex.

	Male			*Female*			*'t' value*
	N	*Mean*	*SD*	*N*	*Mean*	*SD*	
Pre st udy	224	15.97	3.46	285	16.46	3.51	1.57
Post study	224	17.16	3.65	285	17.43	3.74	1.482
	't' value=2.506			**'t' value=3.191**			

The mean scores obtained at the pre study and post study was presented in the table no.1.2.0. The data in table indicated that the male and female students did not differ significantly on their knowledge on "Adolescence Development Process" at the pre study. In other words they were comparable in terms of their levels of knowledge on "Adolescence development Process".

After learning the self-instructional material on 'Adolescence development process', the students of both sex changed very significantly in their knowledge level on 'Adolescence development Process'. The results indicated that there was significant learning taking place through self-instructional material on 'Adolescence development Process' among the students of these two groups.

But where as these two groups were not significant when the mean scores of knowledge at post study. It indicated that the learning among these two groups of students was taking place uniformly.

Hypothesis No. 1.3.0: There will be no significant difference between the achievement (knowledge gain) of arts and & Science subject students through learning of self-instructional material on 'Adolescence Development Process'.

The mean score of knowledge on 'Adolescence Development Process' obtained of pre study indicated that the students of Arts and Science group did not differ significantly in their knowledge level. In other words they were similar and comparable in notice with regard to knowledge level of pre study.

Table 1.3.0: Mean scores of students knowledge before and after studying self-instructional material on 'Adolescence Development Process' by course of study.

	Arts			Science			't' value
	N	*Mean*	*SD*	*N*	*Mean*	*SD*	
Pre study	223	16.09	3.68	286	16.36	3.34	0.85
Post study	223	17.74	3.18	286	18.03	3.39	0.702
	't' value=3.592			**'t' value=4.197**			

After learning the given self-instructional material on 'Adolescence development process' both the Arts and Science group students changed significantly in their knowledge level on 'Adolescence development process'. It indicated that there was significant learning taking place through self-instructional materials among the students of these two groups.

But when comparing the mean scores of knowledge at post study, these two groups were not significantly different. The results indicated that the learning was taking place uniformly among these two groups.

Hypothesis No. 1.4.0: There will be no significant difference between the achievement (knowledge gain) of 17-18 years age group and 19+ years group students through learning of self-instructional material on/adolescence Development Process'.

Table 1.4.0: Mean scores of students knowledge before and after studying self-instructional material on 'Adolescence Development Process' by age.

	17-18yesrs			*19+ years*			*'t' value*
	N	*Mean*	*SD*	*N*	*Mean*	*SD*	
Pre st udy	288	16.84	3.78	221	15.77	3.46	3.95
Post study	288	18.06	3.18	221	17.98	3.66	0.185
	't' value=2.975			**'t' value=4.612**			

The mean scores of students in the age group 17-18 years

age and 19+ years age group were presented in table no. 1.4.0. the mean score obtain at pre study indicated that the students in the age group of 17-18 years and 19+ years were significantly different in their knowledge level. It indicates that the students in the age group 17-18 years were having more knowledge the are of 'Adolescence development process' than the 19+ years age group.

After learning the self-instructional material on 'Adolescence Development Process' the students of both the age groups changed very significantly on their knowledge level. It indicates that there was significant learning taking place through self-instructional materials among the students of these two age groups.

But whereas these two age groups were not significantly when comparing the mean scores of knowledge at post study. The results indicated that the learning was taking place uniformly among these two age groups.

Hypothesis No. 1.5.0: There will be significant difference between the achievement (knowledge gain) of students who studied school education at Rural school and Urban school through learning of self-instructional material on 'Adolescence Development Process'.

Table 1.5.0: Mean scores of students knowledge before and after studying self-instructional material on 'Adolescence Development Process' by School Education.

	Urban School			*Rural School*			*'t' value*
	N	*Mean*	*SD*	*N*	*Mean*	*SD*	
Pre st udy	334	16.97	2.66	175	15.07	2.91	3.0643
Post study	334	18.36	3.42	175	17.14	3.04	2.871
	't' value=3.316			**'t' value=4.072**			

The mean scores obtained at pre study and post study are presented in the Table no. 1.5.0. the data in the table indicated that the students who studied at Rural schools and Urban schools were significantly different in their knowledge level. It indicates that the students who studied in the urban schools were having higher knowledge their students from the rural schools in area of 'Adolescence development processes'.

After learning the self-instructional material on 'Adolescence development process', the students of both these two groups gained knowledge significantly in the area of 'Adolescence development process'. It indicates that there was significant learning taking place through self-instructional materials among the students of these two groups of students.

But where as these two group of students were also significantly different when comparing the mean scores of knowledge at post study. The results indicated that the learning was taking place uniformly among these two group of students.

Attitude Change

Objective

To ascertain the effectiveness of the developed self-instructional material for college adolescents in terms of attitude change in the area of 'Adolescence development processes' through pre and post experimentation.

The Investigator formulated five corresponding Null-Hypothesis of this objective which are follows;

Hypothesis No. 1.6.0: There will be no significant difference between the achievement (Attitude change) of Rural college students and Urban college students through learning of self-instructional material on 'Adolescence Development Process'.

The mean scores obtained at the pre study and post study presented in the table no. 1.6.0. the data in the table indicated that the rural college students and urban college students did not differ significantly in their attitude level at the pre study. In other worlds they were comparable in terms of their level of attitude towards 'Adolescence development Process'.

Table 1.6.0: Mean scores of student's Attitude before and after studying self-instructional material on 'Adolescence Development Process' by Rural and Urban colleges.

	Rural College			*Urban College*			*'t' value*
	N	*Mean*	*SD*	*N*	*Mean*	*SD*	
Pre study	201	9.34	1.61	308	9.12	1.73	1.48
Post study	201	10.67	2.03	308	10.48	1.92	0.614
	't' value=5.179			**'t' value=5.133**			

After learning the given self-instructional materials both the Rural and Urban college students changed significantly in their attitude level towards Adolescence Development Process. The results indicated that there was significant learning taking place through learning self-instructional materials among them.

But when comparing these two groups of students the mean scores were not significant at post study. It indicated that the attitudinal change through learning of self-instructional material among these two groups of students was taking place uniformly.

Hypothesis No. 1.7.0: There will be no significant difference between the achievement (Attitude Change) of Male and Female students through learning of self-instructional material on 'Adolescence Development Processes'.

Table 1.7.0: Mean scores of students Attitude before and after studying self-instructional material on 'Adolescence Developmental Process' by sex.

	Male			*Female*			*'t' value*
	N	*Mean*	*SD*	*N*	*Mean*	*SD*	
Pre study	224	8.99	1.73	285	9.37	1.68	2.52
Post study	224	10.16	1.94	285	10.39	1.96	0.936
	't' value=4.771			**'t' value=4.731**			

The mean scores obtained at pre study indicated that male and female students were differing significantly in their attitude level towards 'Adolescence development process'. The results indicated that the female students were having more favourable attitude towards' Adolescence development processes' than the male students.

After learning the self-instructional materials on 'Adolescence development processes', both the male and female students groups were changed significantly in their attitude level. It indicated that there were significant learning taking place through studying of self-instructional material on 'Adolescence development Processes'.

But when comparing the mean scores of attitude obtained at post study, these two groups were not significantly differed. It indicates that the attitudinal change through learning of self-instructional material was uniform among these two groups of student.

Hypothesis No. 1.8.0: There will be no significant difference between the achievement (Attitude change) of Arts and Science group students through learning of self-instructional material on 'Adolescence Development Process'.

Table 1.8.0: Mean scores of students Attitude before and after studying self-instructional material on 'Adolescence Development Process' by course of study.

	Arts			*Science*			*'t' value*
	N	*Mean*	*SD*	*N*	*Mean*	*SD*	
Pre study	223	9.33	1.72	286	9.11.	1.652	1.49
Post study	223	10.17	1.58	286	10.32	1.74	0.719
	't' value=3.803			**'t' value=6.032**			

The mean scores of attitude on 'Adolescence development Process' obtained at pre study indicated that the students of Arts Group and Science group did not differ significantly in their attitude level. In other worlds they were similar and comparable in terms of their attitude level toward 'Adolescence development Process'.

After learning the given self-instructional material both the arts and science group students changed significantly in their attitude level towards 'Adolescence development Process'. It indicated that there were significant attitude changes taking place through learning of self-instructional materials among the students of these two groups.

But when comparing the mean scores of attitude at post study, these two groups were not significantly differed. The results indicated that the change in their attitude level was uniform among these two groups of students.

Hypothesis No. 1.9.0: There will be no significant difference between the achievement (Attitude change) of 17-18 years age group students and 19+ years age group students through learning of self-instructional material on 'Adolescence development process'.

Table 1.9.0: Mean scores of students Attitude before and after studying self-instructional material on 'Adolescence Development Process'.

	17-18 years age			*19+ years age*			*'t' value*
	N	*Mean*	*SD*	*N*	*Mean*	*SD*	
Pre study	288	9.36	1.76	221	8.98	1.721	1.731
Post study	288	10.97	1.81	221	10.44	1.51	1.823
	't' value=7.650			**'t' value=5.132**			

The mean scores of attitude towards 'Adolescence Development Process' obtained of pre study indicated that the students in the age group 17-18 years and 19+ years did not differ significantly in their attitude level. In other words, they were similar and comparable in terms of their attitude level.

After learning the given self-instructional material both the group of students changed significantly in their attitude level towards 'Adolescence development Process'. The results indicated that there was significant learning of self-instructional materials among these age group students.

But when comparing the mean scores of attitude at post

study, these two age groups students were not significantly different. It indicated that the attitude change through learning of self-instructional materials was taking place uniformly among these two age groups.

Hypothesis No. 1.10.0: There will be no significant difference between the achievement (Attitude change) of students who studied school education at Rural school and Urban school through learning of self-instructional material on 'Adolescence Development Process'.

Table 1.10.0: Mean scores of students Attitude before and after studying self-instructional material on 'Adolescence Development Process' by school education.

	Urban School			*Rural School*			*'t' value*
	N	*Mean*	*SD*	*N*	*Mean*	*SD*	
Pre study	334	9.071	1.561	175	9.12	1.731	0.934
Post study	334	10.32	1.42	175	10.34	1.48	0.0697
	't' value=5.758			**'t' value=3.832**			

The mean scores of attitude towards 'Adolescence Development Process' obtained at the pre study indicated that the students who studies in rural school, and urban schools did not differ significantly in their attitude level. In other words, they were similar and comparable in terms of their attitude level after learning the self-instructional materials. Both the groups of students changed significantly in their attitude level toward Adolescence Development Process. The results indicated that there were significant attitudinal changes taking place through learning of self-instructional materials among the students of these two groups.

But when comparing the mean scores of attitude at post study these two groups of students were not significantly different. It indicated that the attitude change through learning of self-instructional materials was taking place uniformly among these two groups of students.

II
FAMILY LIFE EDUCATION
(MARRIAGE, PREGNANCY, CHILD BIRTH & CONTRACEPTIVES)

Knowledge

Objective

To ascertain the effectiveness of the developed self-instructional material for college adolescents in terms of knowledge gain in the area of 'Family Life Education' through pre and post experimentation.

The researcher formulated five corresponding null-hypothesis of this objective which are as follows;

Hypothesis No. 2.1.0: There will be no significant difference between the achievement (knowledge gain) of rural college students and urban college students through learning of self-instructional material on 'Family Life Education'.

Table 2.1.0: Mean scores of student's knowledge before and after studying self-instructional material on 'Family Life Education' by rural and urban college.

	Rural College			*Urban College*			*'t' value*
	N	*Mean*	*SD*	*N*	*Mean*	*SD*	
Pre study	201	25.35	3.46	308	25.48	3.13	0.42
Post study	201	27.14	3.18	308	27.36	3.42	0.525
	't' value=3.822			**'t' value=5.038**			

The mean scores obtained at pre study and post study was presented in table no.2.1.0. The data in the table indicated that the rural college students and urban college students did not differ significantly in their knowledge level in the area of 'Family Life Education' at pre study. In other worlds, they were comparable in terms of their level of knowledge on 'Family life Education'

After learning the self-instructional materials on 'Family Life Education' both the rural and urban college students changed very significantly in their knowledge level on 'Family Life Education'. The results indicated that was significant learning taking place through self-instructional material on 'Family Life Education' among the students of these two groups.

But when comparing the mean scores of knowledge at post study, these two groups were not significantly different. It indicated that the learning among these two groups of students was taking place uniformly.

Hypothesis No. 2.2.0: There will be no significant difference between the achievement (knowledge gain) of Male and Female students through learning of self-instructional material on 'Family Life'.

Table 2.2.0: Mean scores of students knowledge before and after studying self-instructional material on 'Family Life education' by Sex.

	Male			*Female*			*'t' value*
	N	*Mean*	*SD*	*N*	*Mean*	*SD*	
Pre study	224	25.27	3.37	285	25.55	3.17	0.98
Post study	224	27.12	3.21	285	27.43	3.11	0.778
	't' value=4.208			**'t' value=5.055**			

The mean scores obtained at pre study and post study was presented in table no.2.1.0. The data in table indicted that the rural college students and urban college students did not differ significantly in their knowledge level in the area of 'family Life Education' at pre study. In other words, they were comparable in terms of their level of knowledge on 'Family Life Education'.

After learning the self-instructional materials on 'Family Life Education' both male and female students changed very significantly in their knowledge level on "Family Life Education". These results indicated that they were significant learning taking place through self-instructional material on 'Family Life Education' among the students of these two groups.

But when comparing the mean scores of knowledge at post study, these two groups were not significantly different. It indicated that the learning among these two groups of students was taking place uniformly.

Hypothesis No. 2.3.0: There will be no significant difference between the achievement of (knowledge gain) Arts and Science students through learning of self-instructional material on 'Family Life Education'.

Table 2.3.0: Mean scores of students knowledge before and after studying self-instructional material on 'Family Life Education' by course of study.

	Arts			*Science*			*'t' value*
	N	*Mean*	*SD*	*N*	*Mean*	*SD*	
Pre study	223	25.13	3.17	286	25.66	3.32	1.80
Post study	223	27.18	3.21	286	27.81	3.42	1.029
	't' value=4.798			**'t' value=5.395**			

The mean scores of knowledge on 'Family Life Education' at pre study indicated that the students of arts and science groups did not differ significantly in their knowledge level. In other words, they were similar and comparable in nature units regard to knowledge in 'Family Life Education' at pre study.

After learning the developed self-instructional material on 'family Life Education' both the arts and science group students gained significantly in their knowledge level on 'family Life Education'. It indicated that there as significant learning taking place through self-instructional material on 'family Life Education' among the students of these two groups.

But when comparing the mean scores of knowledge at post study, these two groups were not significantly different. The results indicated that the learning through self-instructional material on 'Family Life Education' was taking place uniformly among these two groups.

Hypothesis No. 2.4.0: There will be no significant difference between the achievement of (knowledge gain) 17-18 years age group students and 19+ years age group students through learning of self-instructional material on 'Family Life Education'.

Table 2.4.0: Mean scores of students knowledge before and after studying self-instructional material on 'Family Life Education' by school education.

	17-18 years age			*19+ years age*			*'t' value*
	N	*Mean*	*SD*	*N*	*Mean*	*SD*	
Pre study	288	25.54	3.85	221	25.29	3.25	0.35
Post study	288	27.86	3.16	221	28.09	3.15	0.578
	't' value=5.616			**'t' value=6.504**			

The mean scores of knowledge on 'Family Life Education' in the age groups of 17-18 years and 19+ years were presented in the table no.2.4.0. The mean scores obtained at pre study indicated that the students in the age of 17-18 years age group and 19+years age groups were not significantly different in their knowledge level. It indicates that the students in the age group 17-18 years and 19+ years age groups were similar and comparable in terms of knowledge level in the area of 'Family Life Education' at pre study.

After learning the self-instructional material on 'Family Life Education' the students of both the age groups changed very significantly in their knowledge level. It indicates that there was significant learning taking place through self-instructional materials among the students of these two different age groups.

But whereas these two age group students were not significant when comparing the mean scores of knowledge at post study. The results indicated that the learning was taking place uniformly among these two age groups.

Hypothesis No. 2.5.0: There will be no significant difference between the achievement (knowledge gain) of students who studied at Rural schools and Urban schools through learning of self-instructional material on 'Family Life Education'.

Table 2.5.0: Mean scores of student's knowledge before and after studying self-instructional material on 'Family Life Education' by school education.

	Urban school			*Rural school*			*'t' value*
	N	*Mean*	*SD*	*N*	*Mean*	*SD*	
Pre study	334	25.55	3.20	175	25.44	3.03	0.94
Post study	334	27.19	3.24	175	27.38	3.16	0.4565
	't' value=6.186			**'t' value=4.156**			

The mean scores of knowledge towards 'Family Life Education' obtained at pre study indicated that the students who studied at rural schools and urban schools did not differ significantly in their knowledge level. In other words, they were similar and comparable in the terms of their knowledge level.

After learning the given self-instructional materials, both the groups of students gained significantly in their knowledge level. It indicated that their were significant knowledge gain taking place through learning of self-instructional materials among the students of these two groups.

But, when comparing the mean scores of knowledge at post study, these two groups of students were not significantly different. It indicates that the knowledge gain through learning of self-instructional materials was taking place uniformly among these two groups of students.

Attitude Change

Objectives

To ascertain the effectiveness of the developed self-instructional material for college adolescents in terms of attitude change in the area of 'Family Life Education'.

The researchers formulated five corresponding null hypothesis of this objectives which are as follows;

Hypothesis No. 2.6.0: There will be no significant difference between the achievement of (attitude change) rural college students and urban college students through learning of self-instructional material on 'Family Life Education'.

Table 2.6.0: Mean scores of students attitude before and after studying self-instructional material on 'Family Life Education' by rural and urban college.

	Rural college			*Urban college*			*'t' value*
	N	*Mean*	*SD*	*N*	*Mean*	*SD*	
Pre study	201	10.71	1.21	308	10.77	1.85	0.33
Post study	201	11.84	1.36	308	11.41	1.81	1.556
	't' value=5.233			**'t' value=3.257**			

The mean scores of attitude towards 'Family Life Education' obtained at pre study indicated that the Rural and Urban college students were not significant different in their attitude level towards 'Family Life Education'. In other words, they were similar and comparable in terms of their attitude level towards 'Family Life Education'.

After learning the given self-instructional materials, both the rural and urban college students changed significantly in their attitude level towards 'Family Life Education'. The results indicated that there was significant learning taking place through the self-instructional material on 'Family Life Education' among them.

When comparing the mean scores of attitude at post study, these two groups of students were not significantly different. The results indicated that the attitude change through learning of self-instructional materials was taking place uniformly among these two groups of students.

Hypothesis No. 2.7.0: There will be no significant difference between the achievement of (Attitude change) Male and Female students through learning of self-instructional materials on 'Family life Education'.

Table 2.7.0: Mean scores of student's attitude before and after studying self-instructional material on 'Family Life Education' by sex.

	Male			*Female*			*'t' value*
	N	*Mean*	*SD*	*N*	*Mean*	*SD*	
Pre study	224	10.612	1.919	285	10.852	1.765	1.541
Post study	224	11.214	1.811	285	11.586	1.884	1.577
	't' value=2.416			**'t' value=3.397**			

The man scores of attitude towards 'Family Life Education' obtained at pre study indicated that male and female students did not differ significantly in their attitude level. In other words, they were similar and comparable in terms of their attitude level.

After learning the given self-instructional material, both the male and female students changed very significantly in their attitude level towards 'Family Life Education'. The results indicated that there was significant knowledge given taking place through learning of self-instructional materials among the students of both the sex.

But, when comparing the mean scores of attitude at post study, these two groups of students were not significantly different. It indicated that the attitude change through learning of self-instructional materials was taking place uniformly among these two groups of students.

Hypothesis No. 2.8.0: There will be no significant difference between the achievement (Attitude change) of Arts and Science group students through learning of self-instructional material on 'Family Life Education'.

The mean scores of attitude towards 'Family Life Education' obtained at pre study indicated that the students of Arts and Science group did not differ significantly in their attitude level. In other words, they were similar and comparable in terms of their attitude level towards 'Family Life Education'.

Table 2.8.0: Mean scores of students attitude before and after studying self-instructional materials on 'Family Life Education' by course of study.

	Arts			*Science*			*'t' value*
	N	*Mean*	*SD*	*N*	*Mean*	*SD*	
Pre study	223	10.711	1.627	286	10.771	1.978	0.34
Post study	223	12.041	1.361	286	11.916	1.814	1.134
	't' value=5.694			**'t' value=6.450**			

After learning the given self-instructional material both the arts and science group students changed significantly in their attitude level towards 'Family life education'. The results indicated that there was significant attitude change taking place through learning of self-instructional materials among the students of these groups.

But, when comparing the mean scores of attitude at post study, these two groups were not significantly different. The results indicated that the change in their attitude level was uniform among these two groups.

Hypotheses No. 2.9.0: There will be no significant difference between the achievement (Attitude change) of 17-18 years age group and 19+ years' age group students through learning of self-instructional material on 'Family Life Education'

Table 2.9.0: Mean scores of student's attitude before and after studying self-instructional material on 'Family Life Education' by age.

	17-18 years age			*19+ years age*			*'t' value*
	N	*Mean*	*SD*	*N*	*Mean*	*SD*	
Pre study	288	10.791	1.936	221	10.592	1.838	0.159
Post study	288	12.084	1.384	221	11.982	1.213	0.826
	't' value=5.595			**'t' value=5.877**			

The mean scores of attitude towards 'Family Life Education' obtained at pre study indicated that the students in the age group of 17-18 years and 19+ years did not differ significantly in their attitude level. In other words, they were comparable on nature in terms of attitude level towards 'Family Life Education' at pre study.

After learning the given self-instructional material on 'Family Life Education' both age group students changed very significantly in their attitude level toward 'Family Life Education'. It indicated that there was significant attitude change taking place through learning of self-instructional materials among the students of these two groups.

But when comparing the mean scores of attitude of post study, these two groups of students were not significantly different. It indicated that the attitude change through learning of self-instructional materials were taking place uniformly among these two groups.

Hypothesis No. 2.10.0: There will be no significantly difference between the achievement (Attitude change) of students who studied at Rural school and Urban school through learning of self-instructional material on 'Family Life Education'.

Table 2.10.0: Mean scores of student's attitude before and after studying self-instructional material on 'Family Life Education'.

	Urban school			*Rural school*			*'t' value*
	N	*Mean*	*SD*	*N*	*Mean*	*SD*	
Pre study	334	10.764	1.807	175	10.834	1.901	1.134
Post study	334	12.018	1.241	175	12.061	1.341	1.765
	't' value=5.791			**'t' value=4.281**			

The mean scores of attitude towards 'Family Life Education' obtained at pre study indicated that the students who studied in Rural schools and Urban Schools did not differ significantly in their attitude level. In other words they were similar and comparable in terms of their attitude level.

After learning the given self-instructional material, both the group of students changed very significantly in their attitude level towards 'Family Life Education'. The results indicated that there was significant attitude change taking place through learning of self-instructional materials among the students of these two groups.

But when comparing the mean scores of attitude and post study, these two groups of students were not significantly differed. It indicated that the attitude changes through learning of self-instructional materials were taking place uniformly among these two groups.

III
SEXUALITY

Knowledge

Objective

To ascertain the effectiveness of the developed self-instructional material for college adolescents in terms of knowledge gain in the area of 'Sexuality' through pre and post experimentation.

The researcher formulated five corresponding Null-Hypotheses of this objective which are as follows;

Hypothesis No. 3.1.0: There will be no significant difference between the achievement (knowledge gain) of Rural college students and Urban college students through learning of self-instructional material on 'Sexuality'.

Table 3.1.0: Mean scores of student's knowledge before and after studying self-instructional material on 'Sexuality' by Rural and Urban colleges.

	Rural college			*Urban college*			*'t' value*
	N	*Mean*	*SD*	*N*	*Mean*	*SD*	
Pre study	201	10.02	3.30	308	10.58	3.08	2.03
Post study	201	11.82	3.14	308	12.15	2.98	0.843
	't' value=3.962			**'t' value=4.547**			

The mean scores of knowledge obtained at pre study and post study were presented in table no. 3.1.0. The data in the table indicated both the urban college and rural college students did not differ significantly in their knowledge level in the area of 'Sexuality' at the pre study. In other words, they were comparable in terms of their level of knowledge on 'Sexuality'.

After learning the self-instructional materials on 'Sexuality' both the rural and urban college students gained knowledge very significantly in the area of 'Sexuality'. The results indicted that there were significant learning taking place through self-instructional material on 'Sexuality' among the students of these two groups.

But when comparing the mean scores of knowledge at post study, these two groups were not significantly different. It indicated that the learning among these two groups of students where taking place uniformly.

Hypothesis No. 3.2.0: There will be no significant difference between the achievement (knowledge gain) of Male and Female student's through learning of self-instructional material on 'sexuality'.

Table 3.2.0: Mean scores of students knowledge before and after studying self-instructional material on 'sexuality' by sex.

	Male			*Female*			*'t' value*
	N	*Mean*	*SD*	*N*	*Mean*	*SD*	
Pre study	224	11.42	3.08	285	9.51	3.24	5.06
Post study	224	12.68	3.16	285	11.14	3.12	3.637
	't' value=3.022			**'t' value=4.327**			

The mean score of knowledge on 'Sexuality' obtained at the pre study and post study were presented in the table no. 3.2.0. The data indicated in the table that the male and female students significantly different in their knowledge on 'sexuality' and the pre study. In other words, the male students were having more knowledge than the female students in the area of 'sexuality' at pre study.

After learning the given self learning material on 'Sexuality', the student's of both the sex gained knowledge significantly in the area of 'sexuality'. The results indicted that there were significant learning taking place through self-instructional material on 'Sexuality' among the students of these two groups.

But these two groups were not differing significantly when comparing the mean scores of knowledge at post study. It indicated that the learning among these groups of students was taking place effectively.

Hypothesis No. 3.3.0: There will be no significant difference between the achievement (knowledge gain) of Arts and Science subjects students through learning of self-instructional material on 'Sexuality'.

Table 3.3.0: Mean scores of students knowledge before and after studying self-instructional material on sexuality by course of study.

	Arts			*Science*			*'t' value*
	N	*Mean*	*SD*	*N*	*Mean*	*SD*	
Pre study	223	10.28	3.26	286	10.40	3.12	0.44
Post study	223	12.14	3.12	286	12.42	3.02	0.723
	't' value=4.354			**'t' value=[illegible]551**			

The mean scores of knowledge on 'Sexuality' at pre study indicated that the students of Arts and Science groups did not differ significantly in their knowledge level. In other words, they were similar and comparable in nature with regard to knowledge on 'Sexuality' at pre study.

After learning the developed self-instructional material on 'Sexuality' both the Arts and Science group students gained significantly in their knowledge level on 'sexuality'. It indicated that there was significant learning taking place through self-instructional material on 'Sexuality' among these two groups of students.

But when comparing the mean scores of knowledge and post study, these two groups were not significantly different. The results indicated that the learning through the self-instructional material on 'Sexuality' was taking place uniformly among these two groups.

Hypothesis No. 3.4.0: There will be no significant difference between the achievement (knowledge gain) of the 17-18 years age group and 19+ years age group students through learning of self-instructional material on 'Sexuality'.

Table 3.4.0: Mean score of student's knowledge before and after studying self-instructional material on 'sexuality' by age groups.

	17-18 years age			*19+ years age*			*'t' value*
	N	*Mean*	*SD*	*N*	*Mean*	*SD*	
Pre study	288	9.86	3.25	221	10.94	2.97	4.99
Post study	288	11.34	3.34	221	12.16	2.54	2.229
	't' value=3.811			**'t' value=3.292**			

The mean scores of knowledge on 'Sexuality' among the students in the age group of 17-18 years age and 19+ years' age were presented in table no. 3.4.0. The mean scores obtained at pre study indicated that students in the age group of 17-18 years and 19+ years were significantly different in their knowledge level. It indicates that the students in the age group 19+ years were having higher knowledge than the students in the age group 17-18 years in the area of 'Sexuality'.

After learning the self-instructional material on 'Sexuality' the students of both the age groups gained knowledge very significantly in the area of Sexuality. It indicates that there was significant learning taking place through self-instructional materials among the students of these two different age groups.

But whereas these two groups of students were significant which comparing the mean scores of knowledge at post study. The results indicated that the learning was taking place uniformly among these two age groups. It also indicated that higher age group students in 19+ years were having higher knowledge on 'sexuality'.

Hypothesis No. 3.5.0: There will be no significant difference between the achievement (knowledge gain) of students who studied at rural school and urban school through learning of self-instructional material on 'sexuality'.

Table 3.5.0: Mean scores of student's knowledge level before and after studying self-instructional material on 'Sexuality' by school education.

	Urban school			*Rural school*			*'t' value*
	N	*Mean*	*SD*	*N*	*Mean*	*SD*	
Pre study	334	10.28	3.12	175	10.85	2.89	1.47
Post study	334	12.16	3.24	175	12.38	2.48	0.601
	't' value=5.385			**'t' value=3.769**			

The mean scores of knowledge on 'Sexuality' obtained at pre study indicated that the students who studied at Rural school and Urban schools did not differ significantly in their knowledge level. In other words, they were similar and comparable in terms of their knowledge level.

After learning the given self-instructional materials, both the group of students gain knowledge very significantly in the area of 'Sexuality'. The results indicated that thee were significant knowledge gain taking place through learning of self-instructional materials among the students of these two groups.

But, when comparing the mean scores of knowledge at post study, these two groups of students were not significantly different. It indicated that the knowledge gain through learning of self-instructional material was taking place uniformly among these two groups of students.

Attitude Change

Objective

To ascertain the effectiveness of the developed self-instructional material for college adolescents in terms of attitude change in the area of 'Sexuality' through pre and post experimentation.

Hypothesis No. 3.6.0: There will be no significant difference between the achievement (Attitude change) of Rural college students and Urban college students through learning of self-instructional material on 'Sexuality'.

Table 3.6.0: Mean scores of student's Attitude before and after studying self-instructional material on 'Sexuality' by Rural and Urban colleges.

	Rural college			*Urban college*			*'t' value*
	N	*Mean*	*SD*	*N*	*Mean*	*SD*	
Pre study	201	13.01	1.52	308	12.93	1.44	0.61
Post study	201	14.12	1.94	308	14.24	1.92	0.487
	't' value=4.547			**'t' value=5.841**			

The mean scores of Attitude towards 'Sexuality' at pre study indicated that the rural and urban college students did not differ significantly in their attitude level. In other words, they were similar and comparable in terms of their attitude level towards 'Sexuality'.

After learning the given self-instructional materials both the rural and urban college students changed significantly in their attitude level toward 'Sexuality'. The result indicated that these were significant learning taking place through the given self-instructional materials among them.

When comparing the mean scores of Attitudes at post study, these two groups were not significantly different. The results indicated that the attitude changes through the learning of self-instructional materials were taking place uniformly among these two groups of students.

Hypothesis No. 3.7.0: There will be no significant difference between the achievement (Attitude change) of Male and Female students through learning of self-instructional material on 'Sexuality'.

Table 3.7.0: Mean scores of students Attitude before and after studying self-instructional material on 'Sexuality' by sex.

	Male			*Female*			*'t' value*
	N	*Mean*	*SD*	*N*	*Mean*	*SD*	
Pre study	224	12.86	1.656	285	13.04	1.299	0.41
Post study	224	13.67	1.814	285	14.21	1.812	2.003
	't' value=3.494			**'t' value=5.565**			

The mean scores of attitude towards 'Sexuality' obtained at pre study indicated that the male and female students did not differ significantly in their attitude level. In other wards, they were similar and comparable in terms of their attitude level.

After learning the given self-instructional materials both male and female students charged very significantly in their attitude level towards 'Sexuality'. The results indicated that there was significant change in their attitude level taking place through learning of the given self-instructional materials among the students of both the sex.

But when comparing the mean scores of attitude at post study, these two groups of students were not significantly different. It indicated that the attitude change through learning of the given self-instructional material was taking place uniformly among these two groups of students.

Hypothesis No. 3.8.0: There will be no significant difference between the achievement (Attitude change) of Arts and Science students through learning of self-instructional material on 'Sexuality'.

Table 3.8.0: Mean scores of student's attitude before and after studying self-instructional material on 'Sexuality'

	Arts			*Science*			*'t' value*
	N	*Mean*	*SD*	*N*	*Mean*	*SD*	
Pre study	223	12.89	1.497	286	13.01	1.466	0.93
Post study	223	13.92	1.561	286	14.24	1.362	1.491
	't' value=4.909			**'t' value=5.734**			

The mean scores of attitudes towards 'Sexuality' obtained at pre study indicated that the students of Arts and Science group did not differ significantly in their attitude level. In other words, they were similar and comparable in terms of their attitude level towards 'Sexuality'

After learning the given self-instructional material, both the Arts and Science group students changed significantly in their attitude level towards 'Sexuality'. The results indicate that there was significant attitude change taking place through learning of self-instructional materials among the students of these two groups.

But when comparing the mean scores of attitude at post study, these two groups were not significantly different. The results indicated that the change in their attitude level was uniform among these two groups of students.

Hypothesis No. 3.9.0: There will be no significant difference between the achievement (Attitude change) of 17-18 years age group and 19+ years age group students through learning of self-instructional material on 'Sexuality'.

Table 3.9.0: Mean scores of students' Attitude before and after studying self-instructional material on 'Sexuality' by age groups.

	17-18 years age			*19+ years age*			*'t' value*
	N	*Mean*	*SD*	*N*	*Mean*	*SD*	
Pre study	288	12.94	1.477	221	12.88	1.591	0.734
Post study	288	14.12	1.871	221	14.28	1.512	0.709
	't' value=5.344			**'t' value=5.776**			

The mean scores of attitude towards 'Sexuality' obtained at pre study indicated that the students in the age group of 17-18 years age group and 19+years age group did not differ significantly in their attitude level towards 'Sexuality'. In other words, they were similar and comparable in terms of their attitude level towards 'Sexuality'.

After learning the given self-instructional material, both the age group students changed very significantly in their attitude level towards 'Sexuality'. The results indicated that the attitude change through learning of the given self-instructional materials was taking place significantly among these two groups of students.

But when comparing the mean scores of attitude at post study, these two groups of students were not significantly different. It indicated that the attitude change through learning of self-instructional materials was taking place uniformly among these two groups of students.

Hypothesis No. 3.10.0: There will be no significant difference between the achievement (Attitude change) of students who studied at rural school and urban school through learning of self-instructional material on 'Sexuality'.

Table 3.10.0: Mean scores of students attitude before and after studying self-instructional material on 'Sexuality' by school education

	Urban school			*Rural school*			*'t' value*
	N	*Mean*	*SD*	*N*	*Mean*	*SD*	
Pre study	334	12.947	1.632	175	12.921	1.572	0.458
Post study	334	13.968	1.821	175	13.681	1.581	1.305
	't' value=5.399			**'t' value=3.589**			

The mean scores of attitude towards 'Sexuality' obtained at pre study indicated that the students who studied in rural schools and urban schools did not differ significantly in their attitude level. In other words they were similar and comparable in terms of their attitude level.

After learning the given self-instructional materials both the groups of students changed very significantly in their attitude level towards 'Sexuality'. The results indicted that there were significant attitude change taking place through learning of self-instructional materials among the students of these two groups.

But when comparing the mean scores of attitude at post study, these two groups of students were not significantly different. It indicated that the attitude change through learning of self-instructional materials was taking place uniformly among these two groups.

IV

SEXUALLY TRANSMITTED DISEASES (STDS)

Knowledge

Objective

To ascertain the effectiveness of the developed self-instructional material for college adolescents in terms of knowledge gain in the area of 'STDs' through Pre and Post Experimentation.

The researcher formulated five corresponding Null-Hypotheses of the objectives which are as follows:

Hypothesis No. 4.1.0: There will be no significant difference between the achievement of (knowledge gain) rural college students and urban college students through learning of self-instructional material on 'STDs'

Table 4.1.0: Mean scores of students' knowledge before and after studying self-instructional material on 'STDs' by rural and urban colleges.

	Rural college			*Urban college*			't' value
	N	*Mean*	*SD*	*N*	*Mean*	*SD*	
Pre study	201	2.48	1.32	308	2.40	1.27	0.68
Post study	201	4.06	1.52	308	4.81	1.48	1.330
	't' value=2.897			**'t' value=5.807**			

The mean scores obtained and pre study and post study were presented in Table no.4.1.0. The data n the table indicated that the rural college students and urban college students did not differ significantly in their knowledge level in the area of 'STDs' at the pre study. In other words, they were comparable in terms of their level of knowledge on /STDs'.

After learning the self-instructional materials on 'STDs', both the rural and urban college students changed very significantly in their knowledge level on 'STDs'. The results indicated that there was significant learning taking place through self-instructional material on 'STDs' among the students of these two groups.

But when comparing the mean scores of knowledge at post study, these two groups were not significantly differed. It indicated that the learning among these two groups of students was taking place uniformly.

Hypothesis No. 4.2.0: There will be no significant difference between the achievement of (knowledge gain) male and female student6s through learning of self-instructional material on 'STDs'.

Table 4.2.0: Mean scores of students' knowledge before and after studying self-instructional material on 'STDs' by their sex.

	Male			*Female*			*'t' value*
	N	*Mean*	*SD*	*N*	*Mean*	*SD*	
Pre study	224	2.49	1.24	285	2.39	1.33	0.88
Post study	224	4.15	1.12	285	4.32	1.41	1.074
	't' value=4.239			**'t' value=5.730**			

The mean scores of knowledge on 'STDs' obtained at the pre study and post study were presented in the table no. 4.2.0. The data indicated in the table that male and female students did not differ significantly in their knowledge on 'STDs' at the pre study. In other words, they were comparable in terms of their level of knowledge on 'STDs'.

After learning the self-instructional material on 'STDs', the students of both sexes changed very significantly in their knowledge level on 'STDs'. The results indicated that there was significant learning taking place through self-instructional material on 'STDs' among the students of these two groups.

But these two groups were not significant, when comparing the mean scores of knowledge of post study. It indicated that the learning among these two groups of students was taking place uniformly.

Hypothesis No. 4.3.0: There will be no significant difference between the achievement (knowledge gain) of Arts and Science group students through learning of self-instructional material on 'STDs'.

Table 4.3.0: Mean scores of students' knowledge before and after studying self-instructional material on 'STDs' by course of study.

	Arts			*Science*			*'t' value*
	N	*Mean*	*SD*	*N*	*Mean*	*SD*	
Pre study	223	2.34	1.26	286	2.51	1.32	0.51
Post study	223	3.22	1.02	286	3.323	1.13	0.74
	't' value=5.763			**'t' value=4.970**			

The mean scores of knowledge on STDs at pre study indicated that the students of Arts and Science groups did not differ significantly in their knowledge level. In other words, they were similar and comparable in nature with regard to knowledge on 'STDs' at pre study.

After learning the developed self-instructional material on 'STDs' both the Arts and Science group students changed significantly in their knowledge level on 'STDs' It indicated that there was significant learning taking place through self-instructional material on 'STDs' among the students of these two groups.

But when comparing the mean scores of knowledge at post study, these wo groups were not significantly different. The results indicated that the learning through the self-instructional material on 'STDs' was taking place uniformly among these two groups.

Hypothesis No. 4.4.0: There will be no significant difference between the achievement of (knowledge gain) 17-18 years age group and 19+ years age group students through learning of self-instructional material on 'STDs'.

The mean scores of knowledge on 'STDs' among the students in the age groups of 17-18 years and 19+ years were presented in table no. 4.4.0.

The mean scores obtained at pre study indicated that the students in the age group of 17-18 years and 19+ years were not significantly differed in their knowledge level. It indicates that the students in the age group 17-18 years and 19+ years age groups were similar and comparable in terms of knowledge level in the area of 'STDs'.

Table 4.4.0: Mean scores of students' knowledge before and after studying self-instructional material on 'STDs' by age groups.

	17-18 years age			*19+ years age*			*'t' value*
	N	*Mean*	*SD*	*N*	*Mean*	*SD*	
Pre study	288	2.34	1.39	221	2.43	1.24	2.18
Post study	288	3.22	1.13	221	3.32	1.18	0.304
	't' value=5.296			**'t' value=4.692**			

After learning the self-instructional material on 'STDs', the students of both the age groups changed very significantly in their knowledge level. It indicates that there was significant learning taking place through self-instructional materials among the students of these two different age groups.

But whereas these two age groups students were not significant when comparing the mean scores of knowledge at post study. The results indicated that the learning was taking place uniformly among these two age groups.

Hypothesis No. 4.5.0: There will be no significant difference between the achievement of (knowledge gain) students who studied at rural school and urban school through learning of self-instructional material on 'STDs'.

Table 4.5.0: Mean scores of students knowledge before and after studying self-instructional material on 'STDs' by school education

	Urban school			*Rural school*			*'t' value*
	N	*Mean*	*SD*	*N*	*Mean*	*SD*	
Pre study	334	2.42	1.20	175	2.37	1.35	1.22
Post study	334	3.38	1.32	175	3.06	1.48	1.48
	't' value=5.960			**'t' value=3.226**			

The mean scores of knowledge towards 'STDs' obtained at pre study indicated that the students who studied at rural schools and urban schools did not differ significantly in their knowledge level. In other words, they were similar and comparable in terms of their knowledge level.

After learning the given self-instructional materials, both the groups of students changed very significantly in their knowledge level towards 'STDs'. The results indicated that there was significant knowledge gain taking place through learning of self-instructional materials among the students of these two groups.

But when comparing the mean scores of knowledge at post study, these two groups of students were not significantly differed. It indicates that the knowledge gains through learning of self-instructional materials were taking place uniformly among these two groups of students.

Attutude Change

Objective

To ascertain the effectiveness of the development self-instructional material for college adolescents in terms of Attitude change in the area of 'STDs' through pre and post experimentation.

The researcher formulated five corresponding Null-Hypotheses of this objective which are as follows;

Hypothesis No. 4.6.0: There will be no significant difference between the achievement of (Attitude change) rural college students and urban college students through learning of self-instructional material on 'STDs'.

The mean scores of attitude towards 'STDs' obtained at pre study indicated that the Rural and Urban college students were not significantly differed in their attitude level towards STDs. In other words, they were similar and comparable in terms of their attitude level towards 'STDs'

Table 4.6.0: Mean scores of students attitude change before and after studying self-instructional material on 'STDs' by Rural and Urban colleges.

	Rural college			*Urban college*			*'t' value*
	N	*Mean*	*SD*	*N*	*Mean*	*SD*	
Pre study	201	13.01	1.52	308	12.93	1.44	0.61
Post study	201	13.82	1.86	308	14.03	1.85	0.888
	't' value=3.398			**'t' value=5.694**			

After learning the given self-instructional materials, both the rural and urban college students changed significantly in their attitude level towards 'STDs'. The results indicated that there was significant learning taking place through the self-instructional materials among them.

When comparing the mean scores of attitude and post study these two groups were not significantly differed. The results indicated that the attitude change through learning of self-instructional materials was taking place uniformly among these two group of students.

Hypothesis No. 4.7.0: There will be no significant difference between the achievement of (Attitude change) male and female students through learning of self-instructional materials on 'STDs'.

Table 4.7.0: Mean scores of students attitude change before and after studying self-instructional materials on 'STDs' by sex.

	Male			*Female*			*'t' value*
	N	*Mean*	*SD*	*N*	*Mean*	*SD*	
Pre study	224	12.86	1.656	285	13.04	1.299	0.41
Post study	224	14.14	1.821	285	14.32	1.364	0.688
	't' value=5.510			**'t' value=5.904**			

The mean scores of attitude towards 'STDs' obtained at pre study indicated that the male and female students did not differ significantly in their attitude level. In other words, they were similar and comparable in terms of their attitude level.

After learning the given self-instructional material both the male and female students changed very significantly in their attitude level towards 'STDs'. The results indicated that there was significant knowledge gain taking place through learning of self-instructional materials among the students of both sex.

But when comparing the mean scores of attitude at post study, these two groups of students were not significantly differed. It indicated that the attitude change through learning of self instructional materials was taking place uniformly among these two groups of students.

Hypothesis No. 4.8.0: There will be no significant difference between the achievement (Attitude change) of Arts and Science students through learning of self-instructional material on 'STDs'.

Table 4.8.0: Mean scores of students attitude change before and after studying self-instructional material on 'STDs' by course of study.

	Arts			*Science*			*'t' value*
	N	*Mean*	*SD*	*N*	*Mean*	*SD*	
Pre study	223	12.89	1.497	286	13.01	1.466	0.93
Post study	223	13.81	1.466	286	14.16	1.316	1.521
	't' value=4.717			**'t' value=5.142**			

The mean scores of attitude towards 'STDs' obtained at pre study indicated that the students of Arts and Science group did not differ significantly in their attitude level. In other words, they were similar and comparable in terms of their attitude level towards 'STDs'.

After learning the given self-instructional materials on 'STDs', both the Arts and Science groups of students changed significantly in their attitude level towards 'STDs'. The results indicated that there was significant attitude change taking place through learning of self-instructional materials among the students of these two groups.

But when comparing the mean scores of attitude of post study, these two groups were not significantly differed. The results indicated that the change in their attitude level was uniform among these two groups of students.

Hypothesis No. 4.9.0: There will be no significant difference between the achievement of (Attitude change) 17-18 years age group and 19+ years age group students through learning of self-instructional material on 'STDs'.

Table 4.9.0: Mean scores of students' attitude change before and after studying self-instructional materials on 'STDs' by age groups.

	17-18 years age			*19+ years age*			*'t' value*
	N	*Mean*	*SD*	*N*	*Mean*	*SD*	
Pre study	288	12.94	1.477	221	12.88	1.591	0.734
Post study	288	14.78	1.621	221	14.96	1.369	0.427
	't' value=6.183			**'t' value=6.831**			

The mean scores of attitude towards 'STDs' obtained at pre study indicated that the students of Arts and Science group did not differ significantly in their attitude level. In other words, they were similar and comparable in terms of their attitude level towards 'STDs'.

After learning the given self-instructional materials both the age groups of students changed significantly in their attitude level towards 'STDs'. The results indicated that there was significant attitude change taking place through learning of self-instructional materials among the students of these two groups.

Nut when comparing the mean scores of attitude of post study, these two groups were not significantly differed. The results indicated that the change in their attitude level was uniform among these two groups of students.

Hypothesis No. 4.10.0: There will be no significant difference between the achievement of (Attitude change) students who studied at rural school and urban school through learning of self-instructional material on 'STDs'.

Table 4.10.0: Mean scores of students attitude change before and after studying self-instructional material on 'STDs' by school education.

	17-18 years age			*19+ years age*			't' value
	N	*Mean*	*SD*	*N*	*Mean*	*SD*	
Pre study	288	12.94	1.477	221	12.88	1.591	*0.734*
Post study	288	14.78	1.621	221	14.96	1.369	*0.427*
	't' value=6.183			***'t' value=6.831***			

The mean scores of attitude towards 'STDs' obtained at pre study indicated that the students who studied in the rural school and urban schools did not differ significantly in their attitude level. In other words they were similar and comparable in terms of their attitude level.

After learning the given self-instructional materials both the groups of students changed very significantly in their attitude level towards 'STDs'. The results indicated that there were significant attitude changes taking place through learning of self-instructional materials among the students of these two groups.

But when comparing the mean scores of attitude at post study, these two groups of students were not significantly different. It indicated that the attitude changes through learning of self-instructional materials were taking place uniformly among these two groups.

V
HIV/AIDS

Knowledge

Objective

To ascertain the effectiveness of the developed self-instructional material for college adolescents in terms of knowledge gain in the area of HIV/AIDS through pre and post experimentation.

The researcher formulated five corresponding Null-Hypotheses of this objective which are as follows;

Hypothesis No. 5.1.0: There will be no significant difference between the achievements of (knowledge gain) rural college students and urban college students through learning of self-instructional material on 'HIV/AIDS'.

Table 5.1.0: Mean scores of students' knowledge before and after studying self-instructional material on 'HIV/AIDS' by Rural and Urban colleges.

	Rural college			*Urban college*			*'t' value*
	N	*Mean*	*SD*	*N*	*Mean*	*SD*	
Pre study	201	15.33	3.71	308	15.10	3.80	2.24
Post study	201	17.13	3.44	308	17.62	3.13	0.213
	't' value=3.569			**'t' value=5.3684**			

The mean scores obtained at pre study and post study were presented in table no 5.1.0. The data in table indicated that the rural college students and urban college students did not differ significantly in their knowledge level in the area of 'HIV/AIDS' at the pre study. In other words, they were comparable in terms of their level of knowledge on 'HIV/AIDS'.

After learning the self-instructional materials on 'HIV/AIDS', both the rural and urban college students groups changed very significantly in their knowledge level on 'HIV/AIDS'. The results indicated that there were significant learning taking place through self-instructional material on 'HIV/AIDS' among the students of these two groups.

But when comparing the mean scores of knowledge at post study, these two groups were not significantly differed. It indicated that the learning among these two groups of students was taking place uniformly.

Hypothesis No. 5.2.0: There will be no significant difference between the achievement of 9knowledge gain) Male and Female students through learning of self-instructional material on 'HIV/AIDS'.

The mean scores obtained at the pre study and post study was presented in the table no. 5.2.0. The data in table indicated that the male and female students did not differ significantly in their knowledge on 'HIV/AIDS' at the pre study. In other words, they were comparable in terms of their level of knowledge on 'HIV/AIDS'.

Table 5.2.0: Mean scores of students' knowledge before and after studying self-instructional material on 'HIV/AIDS' by sex.

	Male			*Female*			*'t' value*
	N	*Mean*	*SD*	*N*	*Mean*	*SD*	
Pre study	224	15.19	4.07	285	15.96	3.53	1.10
Post study	224	17.46	3.68	285	17.74	3.88	0.588
	't' value=4.3841			**'t' value=4.0553**			

After learning the self-instructional material on 'HIV/AIDS' the students of both sex changed very significantly in their knowledge level on 'HIV/AIDS'. The results indicated that there were significant learning taking place through self-instructional material on 'HIV/AIDS' among the students of these two groups.

But these two groups were not significant when comparing the mean scores of knowledge at post study. It indicated that the learning among these two groups of students was taking place uniformly.

Hypothesis No. 5.3.0: There will be no significant difference between the achievement of (knowledge gain) Arts and Science students through learning of self-instructional materials on 'HIV/AIDS'.

Table 5.3.0: Mean scores of student's knowledge before and after studying self-instructional material on 'HIV/AIDS' by course of study.

	Arts			*Science*			*'t' value*
	N	*Mean*	*SD*	*N*	*Mean*	*SD*	
Pre study	223	15.48	3.69	286	16.04	3.83	1.67
Post study	223	17.85	3.71	286	18.13	3.14	0.415
	't' value=2.765			**'t' value=4.828**			

The mean scores of knowledge on 'HIV/AIDS' at pre study indicated that the students of Arts and Science groups did not differ significantly in their knowledge level. In other words they were similar and comparable in nature with regard to knowledge level at pre study.

After learning the developed self-instructional material on 'HIV/AIDS', both the Arts and Science groups students changed significantly in their knowledge level on 'HIV/AIDS'. It indicated that there was significant learning taking place through self-instructional material on 'HIV/AIDS' among the students of these two groups.

But when comparing the mean scores of knowledge at post study, these two groups were not significantly different. The results indicated that the learning was taking place uniformly among these two groups.

Hypothesis No. 5.4.0: There will be no significant difference between the achievement of (knowledge gain) 17-18 years age group and 19+ years age group students through learning of self-instructional material on 'HIV/AIDS'.

Table 5.4.0: Mean scores of students' knowledge before and after studying self-instructional material on 'HIV/AIDS' by age groups.

	17-18 years age			*19+ years age*			*'t' value*
	N	*Mean*	*SD*	*N*	*Mean*	*SD*	
Pre study	288	15.90	3.68	221	15.51	3.89	1.20
Post study	288	17.93	4.14	221	17.63	3.14	0.659
	't' value=4.405			**'t' value=4.499**			

The mean scores of students in the age group of 17-18 years age group and 19+ years age group were presented in table no. 5.4.0. The mean scores obtained at pre study indicated that the students in the age group of 17-18 years and 19+ years were not significantly differed in their knowledge level. It indicates that the students in the age group 17-18 years and 19+ years were having similar and comparable level of knowledge in the area of HIV/AIDS.

After learning the self-instructional material on 'HIV/AIDS' the students of both the age groups changed very significantly in their knowledge level. It indicates that there were significant learning taking place through self-instructional materials among the students of these two age groups.

But whereas these two age group students were not significant when comparing the mean scores of knowledge at post study. The results indicated that the learning was taking place uniformly among these two age groups.

Hypothesis No. 5.5.0: There will be no significant difference between the achievement of (knowledge gain) students who studied at rural schools and urban schools through learning of self-instructional material on 'HIV/AIDS'.

The mean scores of knowledge towards 'HIV/AIDS' obtained at pre study indicated that the students who studied at rural schools and urban schools did not differ significantly in their knowledge level. In other words they were similar and comparable in terms of their knowledge level.

Table 5.5.0: Mean scores of students' knowledge before and after studying self- instructional material on 'HIV/AIDS' by school education.

	Urban school			*Rural school*			*'t' value*
	N	*Mean*	*SD*	*N*	*Mean*	*SD*	
Pre study	334	15.39	3.67	175	15.83	3.64	0.48
Post study	334	17.16	3.12	175	17.94	3.27	1.806
	't' value=5.183			**'t' value=4.039**			

After learning the self-instructional materials, both the groups of students changed significantly in their knowledge level towards 'HIV/AIDS'. The results indicated that there was significant knowledge gain taking place through learning of self-instructional materials among the students of these two groups.

But when comparing the mean scores of knowledge at post study, these two groups of students were not significantly differed. It indicated that the knowledge gain through learning of self-instructional materials was taking place uniformly among these two groups of students.

Attitude Change

Objective

To ascertain the effectiveness of the developed self-instructional material for college adolescents in terms of attitude change in the area of HIV/AIDS through Pre and Post Experimentation.

The researcher formulated five corresponding Null-Hypotheses of these objective which are as follows;

Hypothesis No. 5.6.0: There will be no significant difference between the achievement of (Attitude change) Rural college students and Urban college students through learning of self-instructional material on 'HIV/AIDS'.

Table 5.6.0: Mean scores of student's attitude before and after studying self-instructional material on 'HIV/AIDS' by rural and urban colleges.

	Rural college			*Urban college*			*'t' value*
	N	*Mean*	*SD*	*N*	*Mean*	*SD*	
Pre study	201	16.54	2.76	308	17.44	2.57	2.638
Post study	201	18.36	2.55	308	19.05	3.21	1.902
	't' value=4.857			**'t' value=4.889**			

The mean scores obtained at pre study indicated that Rural college students and Urban college students were significantly different in their attitude level towards 'HIV/AIDS'. The results indicted that urban college students were having more favourable attitude towards HIVE/AIDS than the rural college students.

After learning the given self-instructional material on HIV/AIDS, both the rural and urban college students were changed significantly in their attitude level. It indicates that there were significant learning taking place through the self-instructional material on 'HIV/AIDS'.

But when comparing the mean scores of attitude obtained at post study, these two groups were not significantly differed. It indicates that the attitude changes through learning of self-instructional material among these two groups of students were taking place uniformly.

Hypothesis No. 5.7.0: There will be no significant difference between the achievement of (Attitude change) Male and Female students through learning of self-instructional material on 'HIV/AIDS'.

Table 5.7.0: Mean scores of students' attitude before and after studying self-instructional material on 'HIV/AIDS' by sex.

	Male			*Female*			*'t' value*
	N	*Mean*	*SD*	*N*	*Mean*	*SD*	
Pre study	224	16.88	2.809	285	17.24	2.61	1.50
Post study	224	18.16	3.11	285	19.02	3.24	2.158
	't' value=3.237			**'t' value=5.137**			

The mean scores obtained at the pre study and post study presented in the table no. 5.7.0. The data in the table indicated that the male and female students did not differ significantly in their attitude level at the pre study. In other words, they were comparable in terms of their level of attitude towards 'HIV/AIDS'.

After learning the given self-instructional material both the male and female students changed significantly in their attitude level towards 'HIV/AIDS'. The results indicated that there was significant learning taking place through learning of self-instructional materials among them.

When comparing the mean scores at post study these two groups were significantly differed. The results indicated that the female students were gains more favourable attitude towards 'HIV/AIDS' through learning of the self-instructional materials.

Hypothesis No. 5.8.0: There will be no significant difference between the achievement (Attitude change) of Arts and Science group students through learning of self-instructional material on 'HIV/AIDS'.

Table 5.8.0: Mean scores of students' attitude before and after studying self-instructional material on 'HIV/AIDS' by course of study.

	Arts			*Science*			*'t' value*
	N	*Mean*	*SD*	*N*	*Mean*	*SD*	
Pre study	223	17.24	2.61	286	16.96	2.73	1.17
Post study	223	19.37	2.89	286	18.68	2.16	2.148
	't' value=6.245			**'t' value=5.949**			

The mean scores of attitude towards 'HIV/AIDS' obtained at pre study indicated that the students of Arts and Science group students did not differ significantly in their attitude level. In other words, they were similar and comparable in terms of their attitude level towards 'HIV/AIDS'.

After learning the given self-instructional materials both the Arts and Science group students changed significantly in their attitude level towards 'HIV/AIDS'. It indicated that there was significant attitude change taking place through learning of self-instructional materials among the students of these two groups.

But when comparing the mean scores of Attitude at post study, these two groups were not significantly differed. The result indicated that the change in their attitude level was uniform among these two groups of students.

Hypothesis No. 5.9.0: There will be no significant difference between the achievement of (Attitude change) 17-18 years age group and 19+ years age group students through learning of self-instructional material on 'HIV/AIDS'.

The mean scores of Attitude towards 'HIV/AIDS' obtained at pre study indicated that the students in the age group of 17-18 years were having more favourable attitude than the students in the age group of 19+ years.

After learning the given self-instructional material on 'HIV/AIDS' both the group of students changed significantly in their attitude level towards 'HIV/AIDS'. The results indicated that there were significant attitude changes taking place through learning of self-instructional materials among the students of these two groups.

Table 5.9.0: Mean scores of students' attitude before and after studying self-instructional material on 'HIV/AIDS' by age groups.

	17-18 years age			*19+ years age*			*'t' value*
	N	*Mean*	*SD*	*N*	*Mean*	*SD*	
Pre study	288	17.457	2.721	221	16.783	2.660	2.164
Post study	288	18.54	2.82	221	18.161	2.154	1.218
	't' value=3.338			**'t' value=4.259**			

But when comparing the mean scores of attitude at post study, these two groups of students were not significantly differed. It indicated that the attitude changes through learning of self-instructional materials were taking place uniformly among these two groups of students.

Hypothesis No. 5.10.0: There will be no significant difference between the achievement of (attitude change) students who studied at rural school and urban school through learning of self-instructional materials on 'HIV/AIDS'.

Table 5.10.0: Mean scores of students attitude before and after studying self-instructional material on 'HIV/AIDS' by school education.

	Urban school			*Rural school*			*'t' value*
	N	*Mean*	*SD*	*N*	*Mean*	*SD*	
Pre study	334	17.01	2.651	175	17.257	2.726	0.612
Post study	334	18.36	2.461	175	18.684	2.352	1.037
	't' value=4.826			**'t' value=3.717**			

The mean scores of attitude towards 'HIV/AIDS' obtained at pre study indicated that the students who studied in Rural schools and Urban schools did not differ significantly in their attitude level. In other words they were similar and comparable in terms of their attitude level.

After learning the given self-instructional materials both the groups of students changed significantly in their attitude level towards 'HIV/AIDS'. The results indicated that there were significant attitude changes taking place through learning of self-instructional materials among the students of these two groups.

But when comparing the mean scores of attitude at post study these two groups of students were not significantly differed. It indicated that the attitudes changed through learning of self-instructional materials were taking place uniformly among these two groups of students.

Overall Knowledge

Objective:

To ascertain the effectiveness of the developed self-instructional materials among college adolescents in terms of overall knowledge gain in the area of **'Adolescence Reproductive Health Education'** through pre and post experimentation.

The researcher formulated five corresponding Null-Hypothesis of this objective which are as follows;

Hypothesis No. 6.1.0: There will be no significant difference between the overall achievement (knowledge gain) of Rural college and Urban college students through learning of self-instructional materials in 'Adolescence Reproductive Health Education'.

Table 6.1.0: Mean scores of students knowledge before and after studying self-instructional materials on 'Adolescence Reproductive Health Education by rural and urban colleges'.

	Rural			*Urban*			*'t' value*
	N	*Mean*	*SD*	*N*	*Mean*	*SD*	
Pre study	201	71.78	11.28	308	72.06	9.61	0.4269
Post study	201	73.61	12.20	308	79.02	11.24	0.5576
	't' value=5.8277**			**'t' value=8.2592****			

* significant at 0.05 level
** significant at 0.01 level

The mean scores obtained at the pre study and post study was presented in the table no. 6.1.0. The data in table indicated that the Rural college students and Urban college students did not differ significantly in their knowledge level at the pre study. In other words they were comparable in terms of their level of knowledge on Adolescence Reproductive Health Education (ATHE).

After learning the self-instructional materials on ARHE both the rural and urban college students groups changed very significantly in their knowledge level on ARHE. The results indicated that there was significant learning taking place through self-instructional materials on ARHE among the students of these two groups.

But whereas these two groups were not significant when comparing the mean scores of knowledge at post study. It indicated that the learning among these two groups of students was taking place uniformly.

Hypothesis No. 6.2.0: There will be no significant difference between the overall achievement (knowledge gain) of male and female students through learning of self-instructional materials in ARHE.

Table 6.2.0: Mean scores of students' knowledge before and after studying self-instructional materials on ARHE by sex.

	Male			*Female*			*'t' value*
	N	*Mean*	*SD*	*N*	*Mean*	*SD*	
Pre study	224	75.04	10.55	285	74.97	10.20	0.460
Post study	224	78.54	9.34	285	79.12	10.34	0.661
	't' value=3.7175**			**'t' value=4.8239****			

The mean scores obtained at pre study indicated that male students and female students did not differ significantly in their knowledge level on ARHE. The results indicated that these two groups of students were similar and comparable in nature with regard to knowledge level at pre study.

After learning the given self-instructional materials on ARHE both the male and female students changed very significantly in their knowledge level on ARHE. It indicated that there was significant learning taking place through self-instructional materials among the students of both the sex.

But, in the post study these two groups were not significant in their knowledge level on ARHE. It indicated that there was uniform learning taking place among the students.

Hypothesis No. 6.3.0: There will be no significant difference between the overall achievement (knowledge gain) of Arts and Science students through learning of self-instructional material (ARHE)

Table 6.3.0: Mean scores of student's knowledge before and after studying self-instructional materials on ARHE by course of study.

	Arts			*Science*			*'t' value*
	N	*Mean*	*SD*	*N*	*Mean*	*SD*	
Pre study	223	74.29	10.57	286	75.83	10.14	1.67
Post study	223	78.81	9.82	286	79.10	10.38	0.322
	't' value=4.6784**			**'t' value=3.7762****			

The mean scores of knowledge on ARHE obtained at pre study indicated that the students of arts group and science group did not differ significantly in their knowledge level. In other words they were similar and comparable in nature. After learning the self-instructional materials on ARHE both the arts and science students changed significantly in their knowledge level on ARGE. It indicated that there was significant learning taking place through self-instructional materials among the students of these two groups.

But when comparing the mean scores of knowledge at post study, these two groups were not significantly different. The results indicated that the learning was taking place uniformly among these two groups, i.e. Arts and Science.

Hypothesis No. 6.4.0: There will be no significant difference between the overall achievement (knowledge gain) of 17-18 years age group and 19+ years age group students through learning of self-instructional material on ARHE.

Table 6.4.0: Mean scores of student's knowledge before and after studying self-instructional materials on ARHE by age groups.

	17-18 years age			*19+ years age*			*'t' value*
	N	*Mean*	*SD*	*N*	*Mean*	*SD*	
Pre study	288	75.28	11.53	221	74.74	10.46	0.4551
Post study	288	79.04	11.20	221	78.92	10.62	0.1240
	't' value=3.8976**			**'t' value=4.1687****			

The mean scores of students in the age group 17-18 years age and 19+ years age group were presented in the table no 6.4.0. The mean scores obtained at pre study indicated that the students in the age group of 17-18 years and 19+ years did not differ significantly in their knowledge level. It indicates that these two age group students were similar and comparable in nature. After learning the self-instructional material on ARHE, the students of both the age groups changed very significantly in their knowledge level. It indicated that there was significant learning taking place through self-instructional material among the students of these two age groups.

But whereas these two age groups were not significant

when comparing the mean scores of knowledge at post study. The results indicated that the learning was taking place uniformly among these two age groups.

Hypothesis No. 6.5.0: There will be no significant difference between the overall achievement (knowledge gain) of students who studied school education at Rural school and Urban school through learning of self-instructional materials on ARHE.

The mean scores obtained at the pre study and post study is presented in the table no. 6.5.0. Between the groups, i.e. students who studied in rural schools and the urban schools, there was no significant difference in the pre study scores of these two groups of students. Similarly, the post study scores were also not significantly different. The results indicated that these two groups of students were similar in their knowledge level at the pre study and post study.

Table 6.5.0: Mean scores of student's knowledge before and after studying self-instructional materials on ARHE by school Education.

	Urban school			*Rural school*			*'t' value*
	N	*Mean*	*SD*	*N*	*Mean*	*SD*	
Pre study	334	74.79	10.06	175	76.33	9.25	2.039
Post study	334	78.94	9.62	175	79.32	10.14	0.487
	't' value=5.7944**			**'t' value=2.8829****			

Within the groups, the difference in the mean scores between pre study and post study were significant. It indicated that there was significant learning taking place through self-instructional materials on ARHE. The results indicated that the learning was taking place uniformly among the students of these two groups.

Overall Attutude

Objective

To ascertain the effectiveness of the developed self-instructional material for college Adolescence in terms of overall Attitude change in the area of **'Adolescence Reproductive Health Education' (ARHE)** through pre and post experimentation.

The research formulated five corresponding Null-Hypothesis of this objective which are as follows:

Hypothesis No. 6.6.0: There will be no significant difference between the overall achievement (Attitude change) of rural college and urban college students through learning of self-instructional materials on ARHE.

The mean scores obtained at the pre study and post study presented in the table no. 6.6.0. The data in the table indicated that the rural college students and urban college students did not differ significantly in their attitude level at the pre study. In other words, they were comparable in terms of their level of attitude towards 'adolescence reproductive health education'. After learning the given self instructional materials, both the rural college students and urban college students changed significantly in their attitude level towards ARHE. The results indicated that there was significant learning taking place through learning of self-instructional materials among them. But, when comparing these two groups of students the mean scores were not significant at post study. It indicated that the attitudinal change through learning of self-instructional material among these two groups of students was taking place uniformly.

Table 6.6.0: Mean scores of attitude before and after studying self-instructional material on ARHE by Rural and Urban colleges.

	Rural college			*Urban college*			*'t' value*
	N	*Mean*	*SD*	*N*	*Mean*	*SD*	
Pre study	201	60.91	5.11	308	61.59	5.23	1.461
Post study	201	62.82	5.02	308	62.91	5.12	0.199
	't' value=3.7798**			**'t' value=3.165****			

Hypothesis No. 6.7.0: There will be no significant difference between the overall achievement (attitude change) of male and female students through learning of self-instructional material on ARHE.

Table 6.7.0: Mean scores of students attitude before and after studying self-instructional materials on ARHE by sex.

	Male			*Female*			*'t' value*
	N	*Mean*	*SD*	*N*	*Mean*	*SD*	
Pre study	224	60.96	5.57	285	61.60	4.87	1.37
Post study	224	61.98	5.37	285	62.24	5.28	1.421
	't' value=1.0731			**'t' value=1.504**			

The mean scores obtained at the pre study indicated that male students and Female students did not differ significantly in their Attitude level towards ARHE. The results indicated that these two groups of students were similar and comparable in nature in terms of their attitude level at pre study.

After learning the self-instructional materials on ARHE both the male and female students were not changed significantly in their attitude level. It indicated that there was no significant change taking place in their attitude level through learning of ARHE self-instructional materials. Similarly, in the post study these two groups were not significantly different in their attitude level.

Hypothesis No. 6.8.0: There will be no significant difference between overall achievement (Attitude change) of arts and science students through learning of self-instructional material on ARHE.

Table 6.8.0: Mean scores of students' attitude before and after studying self-instructional materials on ARHE by course of study.

	Arts			*Science*			*'t' value*
	N	*Mean*	*SD*	*N*	*Mean*	*SD*	
Pre study	223	61.34	5.15	286	61.31	5.23	0.06
Post study	223	62.37	5.32	286	62.46	5.42	0.189
	't' value=2.0775*			**'t' value=2.5819****			

The mean scores of Attitude on ARHE obtained at pre study indicated that the students of Arts group and Science group did not differ significantly in their attitude level. In other words, they were similar and comparable in terms of their attitude level towards ARHE. After learning the given self-instructional material both the arts and science group students changed significantly in their Attitude level on ARHE. It indicated that there were significant attitudinal changes taking place through learning of self-instructional materials among the students of these two groups.

But, when comparing the mean scores of attitude at post study, these two groups were not significantly differed. The results indicated that the change in their attitude level was uniform among these two group of students i.e. arts and science.

Hypothesis No. 6.9.0: There will be no significant difference between overall achievement (attitude change) of 17-18 years age group and 19+ years age group students through learning of self-instructional material on ARHE.

Table 6.9.0: Mean scores of student's Attitude before and after studying the self-instructional materials on ARHE by age groups.

	17-18 years age			*19+ years age*			*'t' value*
	N	*Mean*	*SD*	*N*	*Mean*	*SD*	
Pre study	288	61.88	4.99	221	61.59	4.82	1.59
Post study	288	62.64	5.42	221	62.86	5.30	0.467
	't' value=2.0681**			**'t' value=2.6354****			

The mean scores of Attitude of students in the age group 17-18 years and 19+years age groups were presented in table no. 6.9.0. The mean scores obtained at pre study indicated that the students in the age of 17-18 years and 19+ years did not differ significantly in their attitude level. It indicated that these two age groups of students were similar and comparable in terms of their attitude level towards ARHE at pre study. After learning the self-instructional materials on ARHE the students of 19+ years age group changed significantly in their attitude level. And also the students of 17-18 years changed significantly in their attitude level after learning of the self instructional materials.

But when comparing the mean scores of attitude obtained at post study, these two groups were not significantly differed. The results indicated that the attitudinal change through learning of self-instructional materials was uniform among these two groups of students.

Hypothesis No. 6.10.0: There will be no significant difference between the overall achievement (attitude change) of students who studied school education at Rural schools and Urban schools through learning of self-instructional material on ARHE.

Table 6.10.0: Mean scores of students' Attitude before and after studying self-instructional materials on ARHE by school education.

	Urban school			*Rural school*			*'t' value*
	N	*Mean*	*SD*	*N*	*Mean*	*SD*	
Pre study	334	61.29	5.09	175	61.21	5.21	0.047
Post study	334	62.84	4.80	175	62.36	5.32	1.00
	't' value=4.0491**			**'t' value=2.043***			

The mean scores of Attitude towards ARHE contained at pre study indicated that the students who studied in Rural schools and Urban schools did not differ significantly in their attitude level. After learning the self-instructional materials, both the groups of students changed significantly in their attitude level towards ARHE. The results indicated that there were significant attitudinal changes taking place through learning of self instructional materials among the students of these two groups.

But, when comparing the mean scores of attitude at post study these two groups of students were not significantly differed. The results indicated that the attitudinal changes through learning of self-instructional materials were taking place uniformly among these two groups of students.

5

Better Life Skill Education

Conclusion

More than half of world population is under 25 years of age and over 80 per cent of the 1.5 billion young people age 10-24 years live in developing countries. These young people face serious health hazards in modern times. Adolescents are placed at continuing risk by their contraception, STDs and HIV/AIDS, and their physical health related issues. These can endanger not only their physical health but also, create long-term emotional, economic and social problems. It is essential that these Adolescents are protected from unwanted sex, unwanted pregnancies, early child bearing, unsafe abortions, STDs and HIV/AIDS.

A review of Health care system in India and the type of service provided clearly revealed that the reproductive Health needs of Adolescents in India have 'largely been ignored'. The field of Adolescence Reproductive Health is still relatively new in the region. The health services in India have always been targeted more specifically to pregnant women, the infants and children and nursing women. In fact, Reproductive Health in general and Adolescents Reproductive Health needs in particular are poorly understood and served in India. In many societies, despite a recognition that there in an increased in Adolescents sexual activity outside marriage with a probable increase in STDs, unwanted pregnancies and induced abortions, there in often considerable reluctance among service bodies to provide education to young people about sex, reproductive health and contraceptive methods that might prevent these consequences.

Education in general and Adolescence Reproductive Health Education in particular, is being increasingly recognized as an important input for improving the health status of the population and also in improving the quality of life of the individual.

Adolescence is a receptive age when such and other value based Life Skills Education can be imparted effectively. Thus, the early college years offer a good opportunity for providing Reproductive Health Education to future parents. Imparting such education, especially in view of existing social taboos, however, remains a problem. Many studies have shown that in most instances. Adolescents tend to learn about family life/ Reproductive Health from unreliable sources and in the process, pick up incorrect information.

Many approaches have been tried that for imparting Reproductive Health Education, the most common one being the face-to-face interaction. Because of social taboos attached to the subject its reach through face-to-face interaction is very limited. Against these constraints distance education provides us with a cost effective and robotically describes the preliminary results of imparting Reproductive Health Education through the distance education mode using self-instructional material on Adolescence Reproductive Health Education among the college Adolescents. The study involved pre-study and post-study quasi-experimental design.

The study covered 509 (under graduate I year) students selected purposively from 6 urban and 4 rural colleges of Madras University, Chennai, Tamilnadu. Their age ranged between 17-20 years. The levels of knowledge and attitude of the college Adolescents about Reproductive Health Education were assessed prior to experimentation through pre-tested questionnaire. There after, self-instructional material was distributed to them. Three weeks time was allowed for learning the given materials. Then they were given the same questionnaire, which served as the post study, feedback was also obtained from the group regarding the contents, presentation and readability of the material.

The study findings revealed that the knowledge and

attitude levels of the different groups of college adolescents regarding Adolescents Reproductive Health Education were similar and comparable in nature at pre-study and post-study.

It was observed that knowledge gain through learning of self-instructional material on Adolescence reproductive Health Education among the different groups of college Adolescents was taking place significantly and also gained uniformly.

It was also observed that favourable attitudinal changes were taking place uniformly among the different groups of college students through learning of self-instructional material on ARHE.

In the present study, the self-instructional material was very effective in imparting the necessary information as evident by significantly higher scores in the post study. It was also observed that all the students invariably were gained knowledge and changed favourably in their attitude level towards ARHE uniformly which indicated that the material was appropriate for the level of the students.

The results suggested that providing self-instructional materials on various aspects of Adolescents Reproductive Health Education will tackle the problems of disseminating appropriate health and reproductive health information within norms accepted by the society. This approach would be more economical than face-to-face interaction besides having the additional advantage of unlimited reach. It is also added advantage that the increasing literacy level in our country would be helpful in imparting reproductive health education by overcoming taboos and social constraints associated with the subject.

At a practical level, the material can be produced on a mass scale and distributed to collegiate adolescents. It is the time to incorporate these topics/units in the formal educational system in our country. Self-instructional materials can serve as a useful alternative input to bridge the prevailing knowledge among the adolescents regarding the emerging population issues.

It is now being increasingly recognized that knowledge by itself is not enough to convince young adolescents to adopt positive health behaviour to prevent STDs/HIV/AIDS. In fact

Life Skills and Attitudes that young students need to prevent infection with the STDs/HIV/AIDS; are life skills that will be useful in responding effective to a variety of other problems that may face in the process of growing up.

In particular, educational programmes dealing with Adolescence Education requires that students have an understanding of their own physical and emotional developing during Adolescence, so that they can gain insights into their own and others' sexuality to enable them to cope with the problems of their transitional stage. Considering the needs of Adolescents for education and counseling on Adolescents Reproductive Health relating to biological, psychological socio-cultural and moral dimensions, it is necessary to develop and incorporate curriculum units into the school and undergraduate curricular, prepare a well range of learning materials like manuals, hand books, teacher guides primarily for teachers, trainers, guidance counselors and peer group leaders who engaged in teaching, training and guiding adolescent students on issues concerned with their growth development and related problems.

In conclusion, it can be stated that schools and colleges can and need to play a significant role in imparting accurate knowledge, and also assist them in developing skills to act on their knowledge and communicate it to others. Thus, with the advancement of human civilization, human knowledge has increased to the extent that there is an immense need to impart education and counseling on Adolescents Reproductive Health Education to the college students, a vulnerable section of the society and the parents of the near future.

Implications

The 11 to 19 year old age is called adolescence. This is the period of rapid change and maturation when the child grows into the adult. This is one of the most enjoyable stages of one's life and it has to be experienced with joy and friendship paving the way for building a healthy society with good social relationships.

In India, adolescents (10–19 years) number 225 million,

comprising nearly one-fifth of the total population (Census 2001). Female adolescents comprise almost 47 per cent of the total population. The sex ratio in the 10–19 years bracket is 882 females for 1000 males, lower than the overall sex ratio of 933 (Census 2001). Despite evidence to show that the age at first marriage is on the rise in the country, NFHS 2 data reveals that a large proportion of women in India marry before the legal minimum age of 18 years. Gender differentials in mortality rates are evident during adolescence. Female mortality rates are higher, compared to males in the 15–24 years bracket (CSO 2002, SRS 1999). In the 15–19 years age group, 25 per cent of adolescents in rural areas and 10 per cent in urban areas are illiterate. The male–female differences grow with each level of education (NSSO 55th Round 2001). School enrolment figures have improved but gender disparities persist. Girls account for less than 50 per cent of enrolment at all stages of schooling. Rural girls are the most disadvantaged. Adolescents in rural India, both boys and girls, consume fewer nutrients than the recommended daily intakes (NNMB 2001). More than 70 per cent of girls aged 10–19 years suffer from severe/moderate anaemia (DLHS-RCH 2004), and this high prevalence is a major contributing factor towards higher-age specific mortality.

Adolescent fertility rates are high in India. About 19 per cent of the total fertility is attributed to women in the 15–19 years bracket. Also, over 35 per cent of all reported AIDS cases in India occur in the age group of 15 to 24. Age-specific fertility rate in the 15–19 years bracket contributes to 19 per cent of the total fertility rate. Among the women currently married, the unmet need for contraceptives is also the highest in this age group, with nearly 27 per cent of married female adolescents reporting it (NFHS 2 Year).

Incidences of vagrancy, delinquency, alcoholism, drug abuse/addiction and truancy have risen sharply over the last few years. As many as 24 four percent of drug users are aged between 12 and 18 years. (UNODC and Ministry of Social Justice & Empowerment 2004)

Incidences of crimes amongst adolescents have also seen an increase. Crimes against girls range from eve teasing, abduction, rape, prostitution and violence to sexual harassment. Most rape victims are in the age group of 14–18 years.

The National Population Policy 2000 identified adolescents as an under served group for which health needs and within this reproductive and sexual health interventions are to be designed. The National Youth Policy 2003 recognizes 13 to 19 years as a distinct age group which had to be covered by special programmes in all sectors including health. The National Curriculum Framework 2005 for school education highlights the need for integrating adolescent reproductive and sexual health messages into school curriculum. Based on this the National Adolescence Education Programme of NACO along with the Ministry of Human Resources Development is developed.

The government has launched a Programme called the Adolescent Reproductive and Sexual Health Programme (ARSH) under National Rural Health Mission as a part of RCH. This focus on ARSH and special interventions for adolescents was in anticipation of the following expected outcomes: (a) Delay age of marriage, (b) Reduce incidence of teenage pregnancies, (c) meet unmet contraceptive needs and reduce the number of maternal deaths, (d) reduce the incidence of sexually transmitted diseases and reduce the proportion of HIV positive cases in the 10-19 years age group. One of the main problems during this phase of growth is the inadequate calorie intake. The commonly observed health problems are vaginal discharge, hair lice, headache, painful menstruation, irregular and excessive bleeding, dental problems and short sight. Silent urinary tract infection, poor menstrual hygiene is some other additional problems. Psychological problems also arise like emotional disturbances, depression, low self esteem, anxiety over inadequate or excessive secondary sexual development etc. Some of the specific strategies undertaken by various govts are Kishori Balika scheme under ICDS by Dept of Women and Child Development.

Peer education and life skill development through education dept in Tamil Nadu, Maharashtra, Karnataka, AP etc. There is need for a service for providing counseling for adolescents within the district hospital and the CHC. In primary health centers and subcentres the skills to provide counseling both to adolescents and also to newly weds must be available. Peer educator network is also one of the key strategies to meet adolescents especially in marginalized groups like migrants, rag pickers and certain occupational categories, street children and even larger socially under privileged groups like the urban slums or in tribal areas. Helplines and internet are some of the other way through which educated adolescent can access information. This is the period of life when there is maximal need for nutrition.

The major limiting factor in accessing this is poverty. The second factor is patriarchy when intra-family allocation reduced availability for the adolescent girl who needs this the most. There are various government efforts to address this problem. For example the ICDS programme provides for a package of nutritional services to be made available. In practice few adolescents have been able to access this. There have been special schemes to give 10kms of grain every month to the underweight adolescent. This too has been slow to implement. Preventing the marriage of girls below the legally permissible age of 18 should become a national concern. One needs to enforce the Child Marriage Restraint Act 1976 to reduce the incidence of teenage pregnancies. A more positive approach is to promote higher retention of girls at schools. This would also encourage their participation in the workforce. It is important to bring social pressure on errant families and specific communities by women's groups and organizations. Promotion of healthy life styles through sports competition or a cultural programme for youth can also bring positive change. Some activities can provide opportunities for youth to take part together. A health component that has behaviour change communication, counseling and service delivery aspects could be built into these.

Government Policies

The National Youth Policy (2003) visualises active participation of youth, including adolescents, at all levels of social enterprise. It recommends youth empowerment through education, nutrition, leadership development and equal opportunity.

The National Health Policy (2002) has recognized the nutritional needs of adolescent girls as well as the necessity of implementing school health programmes.

The National Population Policy (2000) and the National Policy for the Empowerment of Women (2001) both recognize adolescents as an underserved and vulnerable population group with special sexual and reproductive health needs.

The National AIDS Prevention and Control Policy (2000) recognizes street children and sex workers as vulnerable groups and recommends the inclusion of HIV/AIDS issues in population education.

The National Policy on Education (1986, modified in 1992) aims to equalize education opportunities in the 15–35 years age group, implement free and compulsory elementary education for all children up to 14 years and imparts functional literacy to adult illiterates. It recognizes the role of adolescents in population stabilization and parenthood.

Programmes for Adolescents

- School aids education,
- University Talks Aids
- Training of Rural Youth for Self Employment
- Reproductive and Child Health Programme
- Kishori Shakti Yojana—To Improve the Health and Nutritional Status of Girls.
- Balika Samridhi Yojana—To Delay The Age Of Marriage.
- Nehru Yuva Kendra — Act As Health Awareness Unit-Through Active Participation Of Youth.
- Mahila Samakhya Programme- Equal access to education facilities for adolescent girls and young women.

UNFPA reaches adolescents through a range of interventions and partners, like the Ministry of Human

Resource Development (MOHRD), the Ministry of Youth Affairs and Sports (MOYAS), NGOs and UN agencies. It collaborates with the MOHRD to support, through curricular and co-curricular approaches, the Adolescence Education Programme, which covers sexual and reproductive health issues, gender and imparting of life skills. For curricular interventions, UNFPA works with the Council of Boards of School Education, a federation of all state education boards in India.. Support for curriculum integration will continue through the distance education system (National Institute of Open Schooling).

UNFPA's key strategies are advocacy with education policy-makers, textbook writers, subject matter specialists, principals, teachers, parents and community; capacity building of teachers and peer educators; student activities and counseling; monitoring and documentation.

With the implementation of the revised 2005 National Curriculum Framework for School Education, the framework focuses on ARSH issues, HIV/AIDS and life skills. Its health perspective draws heavily on the ICPD.

UNFPA collaborates with MOYAS to ensure a healthy, safe growing up process for out-of-school adolescents. It stresses on an integrated approach of health and reproductive health education and skill building in adolescents. It focuses on support for policy advocacy initiatives and innovations as well as institutional capacity building of the implementing partners: Nehru Yuvak Kendra Sangathan, National Service Scheme and Rajiv Gandhi National Institute of Youth and Development.

Because when you are going to develop model, you will be talking about peer educator and so on. So there is need a comprehensive programme for adolescents and if one has to develop the programming, then what is to be done as recommended by WHO is to promote health development to meet needs and build competency to meet the needs of safety-belonging self-esteem and caring relationship and to build competency and physical, psychological, moral and vocational skills, as well as to prevent and respond to health problems from early unprotected and unwanted sex, use of tobacco and misuse of alcohol and other substances, accidents, violence, poor nutrition, and endemic diseases.

In my opinion, the existing health facilities must be made adolescent-friendly.. Let us join together and take appropriate action. Let us work with youth, not merely for youth and make them change agents. The challenges are there, but potential is far greater.

Suggestions for Further Study

- Investigate Adolescents' access to health care and the constraints they face in acquiring good health.
- Conduct community based studies on Adolescents "reproductive Health issues among the adolescent boys and girls.
- Use vigorous, in depth and at the same time sensitive and culturally appropriate research designs to elicit data about adolescents.
- Investigate pre-marital sexual behaviour, awareness and attitudes among more representative samples of Adolescents.
- Investigate Reproductive Health needs and decision making authority among married adolescent girls.
- Investigate the levels, pattern and context of abortion behaviour among the adolescent girls and awareness of its legal status.

PART II
Learning Modules

Introduction

More than half of world population is under 25 years of age and over 80% of the 1.5 billion young people aged 10-24 years live in developing countries. These young people face serious health hazards in modern times. Adolescents are placed at continuing risk by their limited access to Information on Reproductive physiology, pregnancy and contraception, STDs and HIV/AIDS, and their physical health related issues. These can endanger not only their physical health but also create long-term emotional economic and social improvement and losses. It is essential that these adolescents are protected from unwanted sex, unwanted pregnancies, early childbearing unsafe abortion, STDs, and HIV/AIDS.

There is scant provision of information, education and counseling the health needs of adolescents and young adults in our country with specific reference to Sexuality, Reproductive health and Reproductive Rights. The ICPD conference for the first time extended formal recognition a concern for Adolescent Reproductive and Sexual Health. It defines Reproductive health as "A State of complete physical mental and social well being and not merely absence of disease or infirmity, in all matters relating to the reproductive systems and to its functions and process."

In the absence of effective education, young people are often misguided and suffer from poor reproductive Health. This is reflected by the following;

- Girls still marry at a younger age although the mean age at marriage has risen to 20 years as compared to 24 for boys.

- 50 per cent of girls aged 15-19 are already married resulting in early conception and high risks of maternal mortality.
- Increasing evidence of premarital sexual activity among educated adolescents.
- Increasing incidence of illegal abortion and maternal deaths associate with premarital sex and early marriage. Around 12 per cent of the spontaneous abortions were reported among adolescents 13-14 years and 9 per cent among adolescents 15-19 years, including induced abortions.
- Adolescents are exposed to non-pregnancy related reproductive health disorders such as STDs and STIs. Girls disproportionately affected.
- WHO estimate as many as 2.5 million Indians are infected with the HIV Virus as of 1994, with 8,00,000 reported cases of AIDS. It is suspected that many Indians acquired the virus during Adolescence.
- The incidence of adolescent rape (between 10-16 years age) increased by 26 per cent between 1991 and 1995. Alcohol abuse, appear to be the main cause of adolescents rape.
- An insidious spread of drug use and addiction among those in the 12-23 years age group.
- Commercial sexual exploitation of children and young girls, including forced prostitution and trafficking is a serious and growing problem.

It is in this context that the need for educational response at the school and college level is strongly felt to provide scientific knowledge about the various components of Reproductive and Sexual Health and enable the Adolescents to cope with the problems of this transitional phase. To meet the Reproductive and Sexual Health of Adolescents, Information and Education should be provided to them to help them attain a certain level of maturity to make responsible decisions. In particular, information and education should be made available to Adolescents to help them understand their sexually and protect them from unwanted pregnancies, sexually transmitted diseases and subsequent risk of infertility.

To guide the Adolescents the Reproductive Health Education, this study is developed which contains four modules to share adequate knowledge and give right direction to the college Adolescents in leading their adolescent life peacefully and meaningfully.

(a) Adolescence: Process of growing up,
(b) Human Conception and Contraceptives,
(c) Sexually Transmitted Diseases (STDs) and,
(d) HIV/AIDS.

The objectives are:

- To provide authentic and accurate information about physical, physiological, psychological socio cultural and interpersonal issues of Reproductive Health to students in order to develop in them proper understanding of the process of growing up.
- To inculcate in them a healthy attitude towards, sex and respect for the opposite sex and responsible sexual behaviour.
- To help them understand the physiological processes of human conception, pregnancy and child birth and also about the contraceptive methods.
- To make them aware of the implications of STDs and causes and consequences of STD infection and ways of prevailing it.
- To help them understand the implications of HIV/AIDS and causes and consequences of HIV infection as well as the ways to prevent it.

I

Adolescence

Process of Growing Up

ADOLESCENCE

Adolescence is simply a transition stage from childhood to adulthood. It is a stage which all young people go through to become biologically and sexually mature. In girls it may start as early as 9 or 10 years and in boys it begins around 12 or 13 years. Adolescence is a time of rapid change in the body, emotions, attitudes, values, intellect and relationships.

Adolescent changes are triggered by hormones of the pituitary gland and the gonads. The hormones bring about the development and maintenance of the secondary sex characteristics.

Adolescents are passionate people and are apt to be carried away by impulse. They can experience irrepressible you or inconsolable sadness, gregariousness or loneliness, altruism or self-centeredness, insatiable curiosity, boredom, confidence or self-doubt. During growing up the maximum change occurs in adolescence.

An Adolescent is expected to

- Become independent of his/her parents;
- Establish a new social and working relationship with peers of both sexes as well as with adults;
- Adjust to sexual maturity and changing roles;
- Decide on future goals;
- Prepare for responsible citizenship;

- Develop a philosophy of life with moral beliefs and standards;
- Develop his/her own sense of identity.

The transition can be stormy or calm. A great deal depends on the ground work laid in preparation for this change.

Adolescence (14-19 Years of Age)

General Traits

- This is a period of rapid physical growth for boys with development of the primary and secondary sex characteristics along with maturation of reproductive functioning.
- Girls at the beginning of this stage are taller than boys. However, the boys outstrip the girls by the end of this stage.
- The needs and urges of an adolescent are sexually oriented.
- Emotional changes are dramatic and are characterized by mood swings.
- The need to be independent and assertive on the one hand and to build up relationships and establish themselves socially on the other intensifies.
- They are preoccupied with themselves and they have the notion that other people's thoughts are focused on them.
- They want to identify with a peer group,. And peers exert strong influence on each other
- They are anxious about their educational and vocational goals.

Behaviour Patterns

- Teenagers are establishing their own personal identities. They have to free themselves from childhood ties with parents and find their own personalities.
- Their emotions are strong and fluctuating.
- Sexual urges may result in masturbation, viewing of

pornographic material or visiting commercial sex workers,

- They can be angry, aggressive and rebellious. They question authority and break rules.
- Boys tend be boisterous and show off their muscle power or uses foul language.
- Little things about their appearance, work or relationships with the opposite sex can make adolescents very happy or very sad. If they do not have much support at home or at college, their sadness can result in depression. Chronic depression may lead to suicidal behaviour.
- Boys are awkward and clumsy. They are concerned about their body image. They are anxious about their height, muscles, body hair, and voice change, size of genitals, erection and ejaculation.
- Delinquent behaviour is quite common at this stage and can lead to antisocial or criminal activities. These may include destroying public property, driving rashly and causing accidents, or forming gangs and challenging each other. Boys feel a strong need to prove their masculinity.
- Sex-related behaviour can also take extreme forms. Shy individuals may avoid any form of boy-girl relationships. Others may indulge in eve-teasing and flirting.
- Teenagers, especially boys, are active in sports and they play aggressively.
- Experimentation is common at this stage, Peers encourage and sometimes force their friends to try out smoking, drinking alcohol, using drugs, and having sex.
- Adolescences display different behaviours with adults and with their peers. When with adults on a one-to-bias, they are more reasonable, understanding and willing to co-operate. But when they are in peer groups they are entirely different and are quite the opposite.
- Ragging is something that can start off as teasing having fun friendly leg-pulling, but can lead to extremes if it does not stop there. An individual or a

group can make a victim's life miserable by persistent ragging or extreme physical and mental torture. Sometimes the ragging itself can lead to death.

How Adolescence Cope

Coping with emotions or situations leading to negative emotions

Anger

Anger can come on suddenly or can be built up because each incident that added to the anger was not resolved at the time. If anger flares up suddenly it is worthwhile to control it and take stock of

- Personal feelings;
- What needs to be done to diffuse the anger and not spoil relationships;
- Ways of avoiding the situation that caused the anger.

It is not wrong to feel angry but the expression of anger should not hurt anyone.

Rejection

Rejection from a peer group is not easy to handle and may leave the adolescent feeling very low and depressed. The adolescent can cope with rejection by;

- Introspecting and rationalizing;
- Not compromising on values;
- Talking to friends, elders or the person who is rejecting him/her;
- Looking for people or areas where one is accepted and appreciated.

Failure

To achieve, to succeed, and to be admired by members of the peer group is desire of all adolescents. Some feel hopeless or ever depressed when they fail or reach any place other than the first. Some highly motivated achievers are poor losers.

To cope with failures one has to:

- Analyse the reasons for failure,
- Accept failure as a natural part of life and not personalize it.
- Set realistic goals.
- Achieve these goals by setting a motivation plan by oneself or with the help of people that matter.

Conflicts

Conflicts simply mean fight, struggle or hostility. Conflicts occur when;

- People view things differently regarding expectations, goals, male/female roles, etc.
- Priorities of values differ;
- Self-esteem or status is threatened,
- Personalities clash.

Conflicts have to be resolved or they can ruin relationships. They may be resolved by talking, rationalizing, compromising, rearranging priorities or accepting the situation.

Stress and Anxiety

Stress and anxiety are inevitable when people are faced with the demands of living. A certain amount of stress is necessary for an individual to function adequately. But when the stress exceeds a person's coping capacity it has adverse effects. Coping with stress would need;

- Maintaining good physical and mental health
- Developing a good sense of humour and having fun.
- Developing a positive outlook on life.

Depression and Suicide

Depression is a state of extreme dejection, on mood of

hopelessness, a feeling of inadequacy often accompanied by lack of vitality, vigour or spirit. It leads to lack of interest in normal activities such as eating, sex, work, friends, hobbies or entertainment. There may be loss of weight, insomnia, an agitated or retarded state of mind, decreased sex drive, fatigue, feelings of self-reproach, and inability to think or concentrate. Continued depression can lead to thoughts of death and suicide. Depression is caused by a combination of factors, i.e. inability to cope with anger, rejection, failure, stress anxiety along with low self-esteem and a lack of social support.

Adolescent Schizophrenia

Schizophrenia is only one diagnostic category for psychiatric problems in adolescence. Schizophrenia is a serious Psychological disorder that is characterized by an inability to function in the day—to-day world. It includes marked impairment in intellectual functioning, bizarre thought process, such as delusions and hallucinations and little or no awareness of the disorder. Schizophrenia accounts for approximately 8-10 percent of cases of psychological problems in adolescence. The onset of schizophrenia is harder to detect among adolescents than among adults. Behavioural signs of schizophrenia may appear in childhood or early adolescence, prior to onset of the disorder approximately one-third to one-half of preschizophrenic adolescents are identifiable as "deviant" during childhood. The likelihood of making a good adjustment is poorer for adolescent schizophrenics than it is for adolescents with other psychiatric problems. Prognosis is—poorer for younger than for older adolescents.

Building up Self-Confidence

Building up confidence in one's own abilities can help adolescents to cope with their changing experiences. Confidence can be built up by;

- Developing self-esteem,
- Developing decision-making skills,

- Resisting negative peer pressure.

Developing Self-Esteem: Self-esteem is how one feels about oneself.

High Self-Esteem Means

- Believing in oneself,
- Accepting one's weaknesses and strengths,
- Respecting and liking oneself and others,
- Trusting oneself,
- Making one's decisions based on what one feels is right for oneself.

Low Self-Esteem means;

- Lacking self-confidence,
- Being unable to accept oneself,
- Not respecting or liking oneself and others,
- Distrusting oneself,
- Letting others make one's decisions as one feels that what others thinking is more important.

To Boost one's Self-Esteem

- It is good to examine one's values. The values one believes in and which one acts upon should not be different. Hence, self-respect and honesty are very important.
- It is essential to make time for reflecting on one's thoughts and feelings. Pursing enjoyable activities and interests help.
- It is necessary to set realistic goals for oneself. Goals should neither be too high nor too low. Planning goals from today to the next month, to the future helps in achieving them.
- It is an asset to develop one's abilities to the fullest and thereby take pride in oneself and in one's work.

Decision-Making

Everyday living requires the making of decisions. The quality and appropriateness of such decisions can affect an individual's well being. Factors that influence decision-making are;

- Values
- Goals
- Resources
- Lifestyle
- Needs/wants
- Life stage
- Standards/expectations

Steps in Decision-making

- Identify the problems,
- Gather information about the situation,
- Weigh the alternatives,
- Think about the possible consequences,
- Review one's values,
- Make a decision i.e. choose the best alternative,
- Stick to the decision with conviction.

Resisting Negative Peer Pressure

Peer pressure occurs when ones peers, i.e. people of about the same age, try to influence how one thinks or acts. Peer pressures can be good or bad. Either of these can influence one's judgment and actions.

Positive peer pressures cause one to;

- Participate in school/college activities (sports, plays)
- Achieve goals (good grades, a good job)
- Keep the body healthy.

Negative peer pressure cause one to;

- Use alcohol or other drugs.
- Skip classes
- Vandalise property
- Have sex
- Disobey parents

- Pick on people for ragging, eve teasing, or other antisocial acts.

Negative peer pressure can be very damaging both emotionally and physically. The need to belong to a peer group is so strong in adolescents that they succumb to the influences and pressures of their peers.

How to Handle Peer Pressure

- Adolescents should know themselves and should be clear about their values.
- Adolescents should know how to make their own decisions.
- Adolescents should learn to say 'No' to peer pressure.

When one says 'NO' to peer pressure regarding harmful behaviour, one usually,

- Feels good about oneself; one's self-confidence and self-esteem increase.
- Gains the respect of others.
- Stays out of trouble.

BOYS-GIRLS RELATIONSHIPS

Students show that adolescents want and seek guidance on how to develop a friendship with a member of the opposite sex. Many young people hesitate to develop a friendship with a member of the opposite sex for fear of being misunderstood or rejected.

When does developing a friendship with a member of the opposite sex become difficult?

This is due to;

- Lack of the necessary interpersonal skills;
- Ignorance about different facets of sexual attraction;
- Social taboo on fearless and free mixing;

- A Misconception that friendship necessary implies a desire for cohabitation.

In a boy-girl relationship, as in any other relationship, it is important to;

- Communicate honestly and clearly to the partner.
- Be positive in outlook.
- Take interest in the partner's activities, lifestyle and background,
- Take responsibility for one's decisions and actions.
- Keep a sense of humour.
- Listen carefully to what the partner is saying.
- Refuse to compromise on one's values regarding sex, experimentation, family or self.

THE SEX DRIVE

A boy-girl relationship is most often accompanied by sexual attraction. The sex drive can be at a;

- Mental level (thought, fantasies, dreams);
- Physical level (sexual urges).

The sex drive is a natural aspect of life that needs to be both understood and controlled. It should be considered squarely and frankly as a meaningful and respectable part of life.

Sex is a basic drive upon which both race reproduction and personal happiness depend. As a drive properly controlled, it becomes a powerful force aiding personal and social adjustment.

Sexual adjustment is part of the individual's total development into maturity. The maturation of the sex organs, sex characteristics and sex drives direct the individual along the pathway of development to adult attitudes, and sexual maturity hel0ps to bring out what is the best, most generous, and most constructive in the individual life.

The awakened sexual drive produces in the youth,

particularly in young men, a certain restlessness of character so that they are considered by their elders as different and difficult. Their moods are variable. They are impulsive. They find it difficult to concentrate their attention on any thing for any great length of time.

The young woman tends to day dreams a lot, and her attention is there by distracted. The young man is usually more interested in physical activities like sports.

The adolescent male sexual urges and drives are more distinctly genital. In the adolescent female, the sexual urges are more diffused and more associated with emotion and day dreams of romantic situations.

Self-control motivated from within the individual is more effective than that resulting from outside forces. The value of the drive depends upon how skillfully it can be managed. This implies that the student has the right to know as much as possible about his own sexual adjustment in relation to the demands of society. He needs to know what is expected of him and why. He needs to become familiar.

With ways and means of exercising control

(a) Sex drive is an impulse related to sex. It is a biological instinct that is necessary for race preservation.

(b) The sex drive is manifested in the following:

- Attraction toward the opposite sex;
- Having 'crushes';
- Going steady;
- Hero-worship;
- Dating, etc.

(c) Some emotional problems related to the sex drive are:

- Breaking up of friendships due to a widening of the circle of friends including members of the opposite sex;
- Guilt feelings arising from masturbation;
- Teasing;
- Inability to concentrate on anything for any great length of time;
- Daydreaming, etc.

PUBERTY—THE SEQUENCE OF PUBERTAL CHANGES

The onset of puberty can vary widely (for boys 10 to 14, for girls 8 to 12); however, the order in which the changes take place is generally the same. The developments happen in the following orders;

Female Body Clock

1. Breast budding;
2. Growth of bony pelvis;
3. Growth spurt;
4. Growth of pubic hair;
5. First menstruation (menarche);
6. Growth of underarm and coarser body hair;
7. Oil and sweat glands activated;
8. Growth of uterus and vagina completed.

Male Body Clock

1. Growth of testes and scrotum;
2. Growth of straight pubic hair;
3. First ejaculation;
4. Growth spurt arms, legs, and penis;
5. Voice change (Growth of larynx);
6. Growth of underarm and coarser body hair;
7. Oil and sweat glands activated;
8. Appearance of facial hair(beard).

The **"Body Clock"** activity is designed to help young people know what signs to look for first, and to reassure those who are expecting all these changes to take place at the same time.

The Female Body Clock

Puberty

- Begins between ages of 8 to 12 and ends around age 16 or so.

- It takes approximately 3-5 years to complete this stage of growth.
- Onset of puberty is consistently 2 years earlier in girls than in boys.
- Females are born with slightly more mature skeletons and nervous systems and gradually increase this development lead throughout childhood.
- Earlier sexual maturation of females is one reason why male are about 10 per cent taller as adults; by virtue of maturing later, males have more time to continue growing.
- Biological changes vary in time of onset and duration, yet these chages fall into definite and predictable patterns.

Sequence of Changes

Breast Budding (First change)

- This starts between ages of 8 and 13 (average age of 11)
- This development is completed between ages of 13 and 18.
- This holds a psychological importance to young female who may worry about its size and shape.
    - It is not unusual for one breast to develop faster than the other.
    - An adolescent girl may worry about the asymmetry that result, especially if she doesn't know that the difference is usually corrected by the time development is completed.

Growth of Bony Pelvis (second change)

- Girls at birth already have a wider pelvic outlet so that the natural adaptation for childbearing is present from a very early age.
- This change primarily involves the wideing of the pelvic inlet and broadening the much more noticeable hips.

Growth Spurt (Third change)

- This usually starts at about age 10 ½ (may begin as early as 9 ½ years) and peaks at age 12;
    - Growth spurt usually ends at around age 14;
    - Any further noticeable growth in stature stops at age 18;
    - At the end of the growth spurt, the average girl of 14 has already reached 98 per cent of her adult height.
- The first menstrual period invariably occurs after peak height velocity is passed (usually one year), so that a girl can be reassured about future growth if her periods have begun.
- The growth of legs and arms is not uniform;
    - Usually the more distal parts of the limbs (feel and hands) grow faster first;
    - This accounts for the gangly and awkward appearance of adolescents;
    - Ex: foot accelerates first followed by calf and thigh;
    - Ex: hands, forearms, followed by upper arms.

Pubic Hair (Fourth change)

- Pubic hair begins to grow between the ages of 11 and 12 (11.6-14.4) on the average.
- The growth is completed by age 14;
    - Kindy pubic hair appears after the period of maximum growth in height;
    - This development is a sign that first menstruation is approximately 6 months to 1 year away;
- Axillary hair appears on the average some 2 years after the beginning of pubic hair growth.
- First Menstrual period or Menarche (Fifth change)
- One lingering misconception—many people think menstruation marks the beginning of puberty when actually it is one of the later events to characterize this stage of life.
- Generally age range for menarche may vary from 9-18 years.

- This usually begins 2 years after the start of breast development (occurs after peak of growth spurt in height)
- First menstrual cycles may be more irregular than later ones.
- There may be a lag in time of 1 year to 18 months ovulation becomes well established (however, this cannot be relied upon the individual case)
- Successive generations have been generally getting taller and attaining puberty at progressively earlier ages.

Underarm Hair and Coarser Body Hair (Sixth change)

While this development is expected, the ultimate amount of body hair an individual develops seems to depend largely on heredity.

Oil and Sweat producing Glands (Seventh change)

- The activation of glands cause the following;
- Appearance of acne;
- Body odor.

Completion of the growth of uterus and vagina (Eighth change)

- Although these start developing early, their growth is the last to be completed.
- The musculature wall of the uterus becomes larger and elaborate;
  - This is designed to accommodate fetus during pregnancy as well as to expel it during childbirth.
  - Cyclic changes occur in its lining (endometrium)
- The vagina becomes larger and its lining grows thicker.
- Vaginal contents, which are alkaline at the beginning of puberty become acidic at this stage.
- At birth, the ovaries is a fairly complete organ;
  - It contains about half a million immature ova—each one capable of becoming a mature egg;
  - The female is born with all of the eggs which she is going to develop-usually 400 eggs;

- These follicles remain immature until puberty when ovulation begins;
- At puberty, the follicles start maturing into eggs in monthly cycles.

The Male Body Clock

Puberty

- Generally, the onset of puberty begins between the ages of 10 or 11.Sequence of pubertal maturation is predictable, but the rate at which the events occur is highly variable.
- Onset of puberty is consistently 2 years later in boys than in girls.
- Onset of puberty ranges from ages 10 to 14.
- Girls reach full height about 2 years before boys.
- In the year in which a boy grows the fastest he normally adds 3 to 5 inches to his height.
- An average boy of 16 years has already reached 98 percent of adult height.

SEQUENCE OF CHANGES

Growth of Tests and Scrotum (First Change)

- Onset of puberty is marked by the initial enlargement of the testes.
- Growth of testes and scrotum usually begins between the ages of 10 and 13 ½ years.
- Development remains in progress through most of puberty and is completed sometime between the ages 14 ½ to 18 years.
- Along with increasing growth of the testicles, reddening and wrinkling of scrotal skin occurs.
- Testes are the male reproductive glands that produce sperms and the male hormones;

- Unlike ovaries, the testes do not contain all the sperms that will be produced,
- Testes are conglomerate of solid threadlike cords called "Seminiferous Tubules".
- During puberty, these tubules increase in size and the cells in the lining of the tubules pass through a succession of stages;
- From puberty on, the testes continuously produce sperm generating billions in the course of an adult lifetime.
- Unlike ovaries, decline in testicular function is far more gradual than ovaries in terms of both sperm and hormone production.

Straight Pubic Hairs (Second Change)

- Usually an early event of puberty, this occurs between the ages of 10 and 15.
- A prepubescent boy may have some finely textured hair but no true pubic hair.
- Later, long strands of slightly curly hair appear at the base of the penis.
- Pubic hair becomes darker, coarser and curlier as it spreads over the scrotum and higher up the abdomen.
- Strait pubic hair appears before the first ejaculation, but pubic hair becomes kindy after this milestone is reached.

First Ejaculation (Third Change)

- This usually occurs about a year after testicular growth.
- The average age for first ejaculation is 14.6 years of age.

Growth Spurt—Arms, Legs, Penis (Fourth Change)

- The start of penis growth spurt occurs normally between the ages of 10.5 and 14.5 years (average age 12.5)
- Age of completion of this growth spurt ranges from 12.5 to 16.5 years.

- A late developer may begin to wonder whether he will ever develop his body properly or be as well endowed sexually as others.
- Height spurt occurs relatively latter in boys than in girls between ages of 11 and 13 years.
- Average age for increase in height is age 14.
- In the year in which a boy grows the fastest, he normally adds from about 3 to 5 inches to his height.
- The legs as a rule reach its peak growth first.
- The spurt in trunk length follows almost a year later.
- Leg growth itself is not uniform; the foot accelerates first followed by the calf and thigh (more distal parts of the limbs grow faster first).

Voice Change—Growth of Larynx (Fifth Change)

- Deepening of the voice results from the enlargement of the larynx.
- This occurs relatively late in adolescence and often a gradual process.
- Voice change undergo two stages;
- Some early voice change occur prior to the first ejaculation;
- Transition into a deep tonal voice comes after the appearance of auxiliary hair and the period of maximum growth.

Underarm and Coarser Body Hair (Sixth Change)

- These generally appear a couple of years after the growth of pubic hair.
- This change is accompanied by increased body and facial hair.

Oil and Sweat Glands Activated (Seventh Change)

- Body odor develops with this occurrence.
- Appearance of acne is also a result of this;

- Body odor and acne are common concerns for many adolescents
- Increased production of androgen hormones accompanying puberty in both sexes leads to an increase in skin thickness and stimulates the growth of sebaceous glands (small glands in the skin which produce oil);
- Often these small glands grow more rapidly than the ducts that lead to the surface of the skin resulting in clogged pores, inflammation, and infection with the appearance of blackheads and pimples.

Facial Hair—Beard (Eighth Change)

- This is an important event because of its social implication as a symbol or badge of manhood.

Facial hair begins to grow at about the time the auxiliary hair appears.

There is a definite order in which the hairs (moustache and beard) appear;

- The first facial hair to grow is that at the corners of the upper lip;
- Then it spreads to form a mustache over the entire upper lip;
- This is followed by the appearance on the upper part of the cheeks and the area under the lower lip;
- It eventually spreads to the sides and lower border of the chin and the rest of lower face.

DEVELOPMENT STAGES

The developmental stages manifest general tendencies but they do not necessarily describe a particular child. The stages may overlap.

Early Adolescence: Onset of puberty, female ages 8-12; male 10—14.

- Starts to move to peers.
- Vacillates between clinging and rebellion
- Strives for independence
- May be confused, preoccupied with body, wonder "am I normal?"
- May experiment with same-sex sexual behaviour.
- Being to think abstractly.

Middle Adolescence: Female ages 13-16, Male ages 14-17.

- Continues effort to establish separate identity from parents.
- Often become idealistic and altruistic.
- Interested in dating, exploring sex.
- Loves intensely, "desperately".
- Continues to develop abstract thinking.

Late Adolescence: Female ages 16 and over, male ages 17 and over.

- Declares independence,
- Establishes a set body image;
- Loves more realistically, develops commitment;
- Peer group become less important, more selective of friend,
- Able to think abstractly,
- Defines life goals.

EMOTIONAL CHANGES FOR BOTH BOYS AND GIRLS

Increased production of hormones prompts sexual thoughts and daydreams in most young people; there is a heightened awareness of sexual attraction

- Release of semen by during sleep, called Nocturnal emission or Wet Dreams is common at this time. It is also quite normal not to experience them.

- Both boys and girls may experience sexual excitement from simply watching or being near someone they are attracted to. They may not understand that the emotions they are feelings are sexual in nature.
- Sexual fantasies are common at this time:
    - Some parents feel that this is a natural stages of development and not a matter of concern.
    - Other parents feel that some daydreams or fantasies are not wrong but others are and like various facets of human behaviour some fantasies need to be controlled.
    - In general, boys and girls become more interested in each other during puberty.
    - While sexual interest and thoughts are common, it is also quite normal not to be sexually concerned, especially in the early years of puberty.

Puberty is a Time of Frequent Shifts of Moods for Most Adolescents

- Discomfort and concern about the changes in their bodies and feelings may cause emotional stress.
- Moods shifts quickly and unpredictably.
- Crying over seemingly small matters is common for both boys and girls and is not something to be ashamed of.
- It helps young people to share their concerns with parents or friends. Often, they find comfort in discovering that others share similar concerns and feelings.

Increased Feelings of Independence are a Part of the Normal Development in Adolescence

- Adolescents experience frequent shifts of behaviour from mature to childish behaviour.
- Relationships with parents begin to change as young people assert their independence, sometimes causing difficulties.

THE CHARACTERISTICS OF PASSIVE, ASSERTIVE AND AGGRESSIVE PERSONS

PASSIVE PERSONS:

- Do not stand up for their own rights;
- Put others first at their own expense;
- Give in to others;
- Always apologize;
- Remain silent when something bothers them.

Assertive Persons:

- Respect self and other people;
- Listen and talk;
- Express positive and negative feelings;
- Be confident, but not "pushy";
- Stand up for own rights without putting down the rights of others;
- Use 'I feel' statements

Aggressive persons:

- Have no thought for other people;
- Put self first at expense of others;
- Overpower others;
- Argue;
- Get what they want at the expense of others.

The Advantages of Being Assertive

- Can say 'No' without feeling guilty;
- Ask for help when needed;
- Avoid arguing;
- Have better relationship;
- Others will respect you;
- Have more friends;

- Feel better about yourself;
- Disagree without becoming angry.

SAFE SEX

Sexual activity which completely removes the risk of infection, unwanted pregnancy and emotional, physical and social abuse is **SAFE SEX.**

Sex with one mutually faithful, monogamous, uninfected partner is advocated.

ABC of Safe Sex

- **A** For Abstinence.
- If you can't abstain
- **B** For Be Faithful,
- And if you can't be faithful, then use.
- **C** For Condoms.

Things that could Help a Person to Delay Sex

- Go out with a group of friends.
- Decide early how far you want to 'go' before being in a pressure situation.
- Decide on your alcohol/drug limits.
- Don't fall for romantic words and arguments.
- Be very clear about your limits.
- When feeling uncomfortable-leave.
- Get involved in activities (sports, clubs).
- Don't go around with people who pressure you to have sex.
- Be honest from the beginning about your sexual limits.
- Don't go out with people you cannot trust.
- Avoid lonely spots where you couldn't get help.
- Don't accept rides from those you can't trust or don't know.
- Don't accept money and presents from people you don't know very well.

- Avoid going to someone's rooms when there is no one else at home.
- Express affection without having sexual intercourse.

Value Building

- Sexuality is a natural and healthy part of living.
- All persons are sexual.
- Sexuality includes physical, ethical, spiritual, social, psychological, and emotional dimensions.
- Every person has dignity and self-worth.
- Individuals express their sexuality in varied ways.
- In a pluralistic society, people should respect and accept the diversity of values and beliefs about sexuality that exist in a community.
- Sexual relationships should never be coercive or exploitative.
- Sexual relationships should be based on mutual trust, honesty, commitment and respect.
- All children should be loved and cared for.
- All persons have the right and the obligation to make responsible sexual choices.
- Individuals and society benefit when children are able to discuss sexuality with their parents and/or other trusted adults.
- Young people explore their sexuality as a natural process of achieving sexual maturity.
- Premature involvement in sexual behaviour poses risks.
- Sexual behaviour must be responsible and self-disciplined.
- Abstaining from sexual intercourse is the most effective method of avoiding pregnancy and preventing STD and HIV/AIDS.
- Young people who are involved in sexual relationships need access to information about health care services.

Test Items for Students—True/False

1. There is no need to make adolescents aware of sex-related matters, as it will promote promiscuity among them.
2. Only indiscipline and bad adolescents feel attracted towards the opposite sex.
3. Sex drive which is a biological instinct must be controlled in accordance with the norm of society.
4. Eve-teasing is the indicator of an unhealthy mind.
5. Increased hormone production is responsible for physical,, sexual and emotional, changes during adolescence.
6. Bathing during menstruation is harmful.
7. Teenage students should abstain from sex until they are married.
8. Attraction towards the opposite sex during adolescence is the indication of an unhealthy mind.
9. One should not succumb to any pressure from friends to do a thing which he/she feels should not be done.
10. Night fall (wet dream) during adolescence is a disease and it should be treated.
11. Masturbation badly affects the physical as well a mental health of adolescents.
12. It is natural if adolescents want and try to be independent of their parents and other elders.
13. Virginity is not related to the breaking of hymen.
14. Adolescence is a period of growth and development among boys and girls from the onset of puberty to maturity.
15. A person is considered adolescent from 10 to 19 years of age.
16. Girl/woman is impure during menstruation.

Key: 1.F, 2.F, 3.T, 4.T, 5.T, 6.F, 7.T, 8.F, 9.T, 10.F, 11.F, 12.T, 13.F, 14.T, 15.T, 16.F.

II

Family Life Education

[Marriage, Pregnancy, Child Birth and Contraceptives]

CONCEPTION

Conception is the physical and physiological process of a sperm fusing with an ovum. Conception occurs as a result of sexual intercourse.

- The semen of the male which contains millions of sperms is deposited in the vagina of the female. The sperms, once deposited in the vagina make their way at a very rapid rate to the uterus and the fallopian tubes.
- As sperms reach the fallopian tubes where an ovum is likely to be found, fertilization takes place.
- Fertilization occurs in five process:
  - The first process is Penetration. It occurs when the outer layer of the sperm unites with the membrane surrounding the ovum.
  - The second process is a union of the content of the sperm head has access to the ovum.
  - In the third process, the sperm as a whole enters the ovum.
  - During the fourth process called activation, the ovum develops a reaction which prevents other sperms from gaining entry to it.
  - The fifth process involves the fusion of nuclear

materials from the two sex cells after which cell division takes place.

- After fertilization, the fertilized ovum which has become a zygote travels from the fallopian tube to the uterus.
- Fertilization usually occurs in one of the fallopian tubes.
- As the fertilized ovum—now a single cell—moves toward the uterus, it begins to divide, a process called MITOSIS.
- The single cell divides into two cells, then four, then eight and so on three to give days after fertilization, the zygote reaches the uterus.
- Implantation of the embryo occurs 7 to 8 days after fertilization. Now the cells multiply rapidly. This mass of cells is called the EMBRYO upto about 8 weeks from the time of conception.
- The period of embryonic development is a sensitive time for the health and normal growth of a human organism.

PREGNANCY

Pregnancy is the process in which a fertilized egg, or ovum, develops into a fully formed human baby, ready to be born. During pregnancy, which lasts about 9 months, or 38 weeks the fertilized egg is carried in the pregnant woman's uterus.

Signs and Symptoms at Various Stages of Pregnancy

On conception, women experience the common signs and symptoms of pregnancy which may vary and occur earlier or later in different women.

Early Stage

- Amenorrhoea—menstruation stops.
- Nausea—feeling of wanting to throw up, commonly experienced on rising in the morning or even in the evening.

Mid-term Stage

- Frequent micturition—urinating frequently.
- Enlargement of the breasts with darkening of the nipples.
- Enlargement of the abdomen and uterus is palpable.
- Quickening—fetal, movement felt
- Breast changes are more pronounced and secretion of milk (build up of colostrums) is present.

Late Stage

- Uterus has very much increased in size and fetal parts and movements felt
- Fetus becomes viable, that is capable of an independent existence.

Stages of Pregnancy

First Trimester (3 months)

During this period (i.e 1 to 12 weeks) the cells of the embryo begin to differentiate to form specific tissues and organs. The amniotic sac, a membrane filled with Amniotic fluid, forms to protect the embryo from injury. Also at this time, the placenta forms on the wall of the uterus. The placenta is a disk-shaped mass of blood vessels and tissue that transfer oxygen and nutrients fetus from the mother's blood. The fetus is attached to the placenta by the umbilical cord, a rope like bundle of blood vessels. By the end of the first trimester (12 weeks) the fetus is about 3 inches to 4 inches (8 to 10 cm) long and weighs less than an ounce (28 g). It has a head, a spinal cord, limbs and a beating heart.

Second Trimester (13 to 27 weeks)

During the second trimester, from 13 to 27 weeks the pregnant woman usually feels healthy and energetic. She will usually begin to gain weight steadily during this time. The fetus grows to about 12 to 14 inches (30 to 36 cm) in length and weighs 2 pounds (1 kg). The women can feels the fetus moving (quickening) at about 16 to 20 weeks. By then the fetus has developed the beginnings of facial features, internal organs, and sex organs.

Third Trimester (28 weeks onwards)

The fetus grows most rapidly during the third trimester, from week 28 onward. By the time it reaches full term, it weighs an average of 7 pounds (3kg) and all of its organs are fully developed during the last phase of pregnancy, the woman may become very uncomfortable and tire easily. Because the growing fetus is pushing on the women's internal organs, she may have to urinate frequently and may experience indigestion. Her feet and ankles may become swollen at this time. Shortly before birth, if it has not already done so, the fetus usually turns upside down in the uterus, and the head partially enters the birth canal. The childbirth process begins when the amniotic sac ruptures and the woman goes into labour. Powerful contractions of the uterus force the baby down and through the birth canal, or vagina.

Unusual Pregnancy

Ectopic Pregnancy

Sometimes the embryo does not get implanted in the uterus but the fertilized ovum in the tube gets implanted in the fallopian tube instead of proceeding to the uterus. This is called a Tubal pregnancy or an Ectopic Pregnancy.

Ovarian Pregnancy: Very rarely fertilization may occur in the ovary itself and continue.

<Tl Both these pregnancies cannot go to full term but burst in the abdominal cavity within 10 to 20 days of fertilization and cause hemorrhage inside the abdomen.

- Such pregnancies can endanger the mother's life if not attended to immediately.

CHILD BIRTH

It is the process that moves a fetus from the uterus of the mother through the vagina, or birth canal, and into the world. The process normally begins after about 38 weeks of pregnancy and generally lasts 12 hours or longer for woman having their first babies and 7 to 8 hours for subsequent babies.

The signal that the birth process is under way is the start of contractions, and the uterus begins to tighten and relax in a rhythmic pattern. These muscular contractions are called labour. They serve to dilate or open the cervix and move the fetus down the birth canal.

The Stages of Labour

It is divided into three stages that blend into one another.

- The first and longest stage of labour involves the opening of the cervix. It begins when contractions become regular and continues until the cervix is fully dilated to about 4 inches. The membrane that enclosed the fetus in the uterus usually breaks during this stage, and amniotic fluid flows into the vagina to help lubricate the passage of the fetus.
- The second stage of labour begins when the cervix is fully dilated, and it continues through birth. This stage can last from a few minutes to a few hours. During this stage a series of hard contraction of the uterus and abdominal muscles push the baby past the cervix and through birth canal. The mother is urged to coordinate her pushing with each contraction, so that the combined forces of the contractions and pushing work together. As the head emerges, the tissues around the vagina become stretched. If it seems that the vaginal opening will not allow enough room for the baby to pass, the doctor may give the women a local anesthetic and perform and EPISIOTOMY. This is an incision made at the lower end of the vagina to enlarge the opening for delivery. At the conclusion of the second stage doctor stands ready to guide the baby's head gently as it emerges and deliver the baby after one or two breaks, the baby may give his or her first cry. The baby is usually placed on the mother's abdomen, and

after about a minute, the umbilical cord is clamped and cut.

- The third stage of labour follows the birth of the baby. The uterus continues to contract and the placenta slowly separates from the wall of the uterus and pass through the vagina. Finally any tears or incisions in the woman's body are cleaned and stitched.

STERILITY AND INFERTILITY

Sterility is a condition where a man or a woman is unable to produce a child.

Infertility is the temporary inability of a man to impregnate his partner or of a woman to conceive or to bear a child.

Probable causes of infertility are:

- Quality of semen—the sperms may not be properly formed; or they may be immaturely developed, or insufficient in number.
- Mumps—can damage the testicles and lead to lack of sperm production.
- Increased heat due to high fever or work environment which reduces sperm production.
- Radiation—affects the production of ova and sperms.
- Emotional stress.
- Reproductive Tract Infection or Uterine problems.
- Non-consummation of the marriage.

In case a couple is unable to have children it is very necessary that both the man and the woman go for medical examination as the fault may be with both or either of the partners. They should take the advice of a gynecologist or a consultant and follow the medical treatment advised. Scientific advances have made it possible for infertile couples to have a baby.

DETERMINANT OF THE SEX OF THE BABY

All cells in human body contain 2 x 23 = 46 chromosomes. The sperm contains 23 chromosomes and so does the ovum. One of the 23 chromosomes is a sex chromosome which is named as X or Y chromosome. Whereas Sperms have both X and Y chromosomes, Ova have only X chromosomes. The sex of the baby is determined by the way the ovum is fertilized. If the ovum which has only X chromosome is fertilized by the Y chromosome of the sperm, a male baby will be born. But if the ovum is fertilized by the X chromosome of the sperm, a female baby will be born.

The determination of the sex of the baby, therefore, is dependent on the male sperm and not on the female ovum or egg.

HEALTH IMPLICATIONS OF ADOLESCENT PREGNANCY

Adolescent pregnancy, whether within marriage or outside it, leads to serious consequences;

- Teenagers are more likely to suffer from anemia during their pregnancies.
- Teenagers experience a higher incidence of toxemia, which in its most serious forms may result in high blood pressure, seizures, and sometimes death.
- There is a greater likelihood of prolonged labour, which multiplies the hazards to the mother and her child.
- Pregnancy at an early age, before the adolescent mother is physically fully developed, can result in severe damage of the reproductive tract.
- The babies born to adolescent mothers generally have low birth weight.
- The babies born to adolescent mother are more likely to suffer from birth—related defects such as mental retardation, deafness, cerebral palsy, seizure disorders, blindness, and other congenital anomalies.
- Adolescents who begin childbearing in their early reproductive years increase the available period for childbearing. It increase the risk of maternal and child morbidity and mortality.

- Adolescent's pregnancy has serious psychological, social and economic consequences also. The psychological strain on the mother adversely affects her and also her baby.

SAFE MOTHERHOOD

In India women are 100 times more likely to die due to pregnancy than women in developing countries. In India more than one lakh women die annually for reasons related to pregnancy. Major causes of maternal death in India are;

- Haemorrhage
- Sepsis
- Anemia
- Obstructed labour
- Toxaemia

Fortunately most of them are preventable.

The period of pregnancy extend from the time of conception to 42 days after delivery. During this period the progress is not uniform. Therefore, the total period of pregnancy has been divided into three periods;

- The ante natal
- The natal
- The post natal

Each Period has its Own Special Feature and Specific Risk

Ante Natal Period

The ante natal period is the period from conception to the onset of labour. To provide adequate care during this period it is necessary to first recognize the signs of pregnancy. These are;

- Missing menstrual period
- Morning sickness

- Increase urination
- Breast changes.

The common risk factors during the antenatal period are;

- Women less than 15 years age
- 1st pregnancy
- 4th pregnancy onwards
- Previous abortion
- Difficulty in conception
- Unwanted pregnancy.

Every pregnant woman must:

- Rest and not do heavy work
- Take one extra meal every day. The food should contain green leafy egerables, pulses, fruits and milk.
- Tea should not be taken within one hour of taking food.
- No fast should be observed during pregnancy
- Take two tetanus injections at the interval of atleast one-month.
- Must take iron tablet for 100 days.

It is important to recognize the danger signs. They are;

- Bleeding.
- Loss of movements of fetus.
- High blood pressure.
- Swelling of feet and face.
- Hemoglobin less than 7%
- Previous still birth.

Natal Period

Natal period starts from the onset of labour till the delivery is complete. It is safest to have delivery in an institution with appropriate medical facility. In case this is not possible deliveries must be assisted by trained personnel preferably by

ANM or atleaset trained birth attendant. During delivery one must look to the following danger signs;

- Excessive bleeding
- Women in labour for more than 12 hours
- Placement not delivered till 30 minutes
- Child not crying at birth
- Yellowish skin colour of the child.

In such case, the mother and the new-born must be taken to the hospital without delay.

Post Natal Period:

The post natal period starts from delivery of placenta to 42 days. During this period the new mother and baby is vulnerable to new sets of risks. They are physically weak and need rest and proper nutrition to recover from the labour.

Brease Feeding:

- Start immediately after birth even before the placenta is out.
- Feed on demand during the day as well as at night.
- Feed should be given every 2-3 hours or at least 7 times per day
- Do not stop breast-feeding if the baby or the mother is sick.

After delivery look for the following danger signs:

- Fever
- Bad smelling discharge
- Pain in passing urine
- Abnormal pain
- Abnormal behavour
- Painful and swollen legs
- Painful breasts.

If any of these conditions are seen or felt, she should be taken to a doctor. These conditions need medical interventions.

General Precautions

It is important for all women in reproductive age to ensure good health during the pre-pregnant period for healthy outcome of pregnancy. Some of the important issues are;

1. *Timing of Pregnancy*: Pregnancy below the age of 19 years is not safe and should be avoided. Family planning is therefore essential part of safe motherhood.
2. *Nutrition*: The nutrition status of the woman should be adequate before she become pregnant. Therefore, all adolescent girls and women in reproductive age should be given adequate iron rich food.
3. *Personal Hygiene*: Women due to their anatomical structure are more vulnerable to urinary tract and reproductive tract infections. These are easily be prevented by practicing personal hygiene. Hence all girls and women should be taught to adopt hygienic practice.

ABORTION

Abortion is the termination of pregnancy before the fetus reaches the stage of viability. Viability involves the development of the fetus upto 24 weeks or 6 months approximately.

Spontaneous Abortion

This is an abrupt termination of pregnancy within 20 weeks of conception or when the weight of the fetus is less than 500 grams. The cause may be known or unknown. This type of abortion is also called a 'Mincarriage'.

Induced Abortion

- This is brought on intentionally by the use of drugs, instruments, injections, or other means.

- When the mental or physical health of the mother is endangered by the continuation of pregnancy, or if the fetus has a severe malfunctioning condition, then the pregnancy is terminated medically.
- In India, the Medical Termination of Pregnancy (MTP) Act of 1971 allows a pregnancy to be terminated by a registered medical practioner at a recognized clinic or hospital certified by the state government.
- MTP can be sought within weeks of pregnancy under the following condition:
  - The continuance of pregnancy would involve a risk to the life of pregnant woman
  - The serious genetic disability of the fetus or a substantial risk
  - The pregnancy is due to rape or sexual abuse
  - When the woman is over eighteen years of age her consent is necessary for an abortion. If she is under eighteen years of age or mentally deficient, the written consent of her parents or guardian is essential for terminating the pregnancy.

Risks and Complications of Abortion

As with any medical procedure, an abortion is associated with possible risk and complications. These could be:

Infection:	This is one of the more important complications. Even through sterile instruments and antiseptics are uses, bacteria sometimes travel into the uterus.
Retained tissue:	Occassionally some tissues get left behind inside the uterus. This may cause heavy bleeding, cramps, or infection.
Haemorrhage:	Excessive bleeding from the uterus is due to retained tissue, or perforation of the uterus by the curette during the operation.
Secondary sterility:	This can occur due to tubal blockage by infection.

CONTRACEPTIVES

Couples can avoid unwanted pregnancies by using contraceptives. Contraceptives can be used at various stages of reproductive life. Currently, the following methods are available to the acceptors of family planning to limit their family size.

Spacing Methods

1. Condom—for males
2. Oral Pill—for females
3. IUD—for females

Terminal Methods

1. Vasectomy—for males
2. Tubectomy—for females.

TEST ITEMS FOR STUDENTS TRUE/FALSE (T/F)

1. Abortion (MTP) is legal in India
2. Teenage pregnancy causes no risk to the life of mother.
3. Sterilsation reduces sexual desire and capacity of men and women.
4. Hysterectomy terminates women's sex life.
5. If a man is sterilized, he will not be able to perform sexually. He will be like castrated bull.
6. Absence or deficiency of sperms affects one's potency.
7. Safe sex should be taught to all adolescents.
8. Getting authentic knowledge about sex-related issues increase sexual urge and is against mortality.
9. Teenage girls have very low risk of miscarriage and birth defects in their babies as compared to woman in other age groups.
10. A woman can get pregnant the first time she has sexual relation with a man.
11. Girls can get pregnant even if she has sex once.

12. Smoking and drinking during pregnancy increase the risk of birth defects and other problems for the child.
13. One drop of semen equal to 100 drops of blood.
14. It is okay for a boy to have premarital sex, but a girl should be a virgin when she gets married.
15. Menopause is the end of sex life.

Key: 1.T, 2.F 3.F 4.F 5.F 6.F 7.T 8.F 9.F 10.T 11.T 12.T 13.F 14. F15.F

III

Sexually Transmitted Diseases (STDs)

INTRODUCTION

- STD stands for Sexually Transmitted Disease. STDs are a group of communicable diseases that are predominately transmitted by sexual contact with an infected person.
- STDs are also known as veneral diseases (V.D)
- STDs are caused by a variety of bacterias, viruses, fungus, protozoa etc.
- There are more than 20 STDs. Some of the more common STDs are;
  - Gonorrhea
  - Syphilis
  - Chancroid
  - Chlamydia
  - Candidiasis
  - Granuloma Inguinale
  - Non-Gonococcal Urethritis (NGU)
  - Trichomoniasis
  - Herpes Genitals

AIDS

A person becomes infected with STDs when he/she has unprotected sexual contact with an infected person, the germs are transmitted from infected partner to the uninfected person through the mucus membrane of the genital organs. These germs after a variable period of time (which is called incubation period and which differs from disease to disease) start producing signs and symptoms.

Common Symptoms and Signs of the Widely Prevalent Standards

General (Occur both in Males and Females)

- Burning/pain during urination or defecation, increased frequency of urination.
- Single or multiple blisters and open sores (ulcers) on the genitals painful or nonpainful.
- Swollen and/or painful glands in the groin.
- Itching or tingling sensation in the genital areas.
- No ichy rashes on the body.
- Warts in the genital area.
- Sores in the mouth.
- Nodules under the skin.
- Flu like symptoms (headache, lethargy, vomiting, fever etc.)

Females

- Unusual vaginal discharge or foul smell from the vagina.
- Pain in the lower abdomen—between the navel and sex organs.
- Burning/itching in and around vagina.
- Irregular bleeding from the genital tract.
- When having sex, pain deep in the vagina.

Males

- A drip or discharge from the penis.
- It is important to note that some STDs may not produce any signs/symptoms particularly in females e.g. Gonorrhea, Cancroids, Herpes etc. Therefore, they act as carriers i.e. they have the infection and can spread it to others but they are healthy.

- One can't recognize a person having STD just by looking at him.
- A person can have more than one STD at the same time.
- A person can get a STD even after a single unprotected sexual ct wsith in infected partner

There may be various complications due to STDs, if proper treatment is not given. They include;

- Complications of pregnancy—congenital syphilis leading to stillbirth. Other STD infections may be responsible for other birth defects.
- Complications in infants—infection with gonorrhea causing blindness, other complications are conjunctivitis (an eye infection) and pneumonia.
- Complications in others—infertility, hepatitis, dementia and cancer.

PREVENTION AND TREATMENT OF STDS

Abstinence is a fool-proof method of preventing STDs, but a really difficult one.

The following guidelines can do much to prevent STDs;

- Avoid sex with partners who have genital rashes, redness, sores discharges.
- Stay way from casual relationships
- Reduce the number of your partners as much as possible.
- Use condoms.
- Urinate and wash the genital area after intercourse. This helps in avoiding some genital infections.
- Prevention of STDs would also reduce the risk of HIV transmission.
- Early treatment is always desirable to prevent complications and further spread of infection.
- Most STDs can be cured if correct treatment is given.

- Early diagnosis and treatment of STDs would prevent HIV Transmission.

Signs and Symptoms of Sexually Transmitted Diseases (STDs)

STD can be caused by bacteria, fungi or protozoa. Details of specific sexually transmitted diseases are given below.

Gonorrhea

Cause: Bacterium (Neisseria gonorrhea)

Symptoms

- Some men and most women have no symptoms. Those who do have symptoms show them 2 to 21 days after sexual contact.
- Burning or pain when urinating or having a bowel movement.

Women

- Thick, yellow or white discharge from the vagina.
- Spotting after intercourse.
- More pain than usual during periods.
- Abnormal menstruation.
- Cramps and pain in the lower abdomen.

Men:

- Thick yellow or white drip from penis.

Mode of Transmission

- Spread during sexual contact with someone who has gonorrhea.

Consequence if Left Untreated

- Gonorrhea can spread to one's sexual partner(s)
- A mother can give it to her baby during childbirth, causing blindness.
- The infection can damage the reproductive organs. Both men and women may no longer be able to have children.

- Can cause pelvic inflammatory disease (PID) in women.
- Can cause urethral stricture in men.
- Can cause heart trouble, skin disease and arthritis.

Syphilis

Cause: Syphilis is caused by a spiral shaped organism called Treponema Pallidum.

Symptoms

1. Primary Stage

- Symptoms appear three to four weeks after sexual contact with an infected partner.
- A painless, reddish-brown sore on the mouth or sex organs which lasts 1 to 5 weeks. When the sore disappears, the person is syphilitic.

2. Secondary Stage

- Symptoms appear 6 weeks to 6 months after the sore disappears.
- A rash anywhere on the body.
- Fever
- Arthritis,
- Jaundice (hepatitis)
- Enlarged lymph nodes.
- Flu-like feelings.
- When the rash and flu-like feelings disappear, the person is still syphilitic.

3. Tertiary Stage

- This stage lasts three to twenty years.
- This is the stage where the permanent damage to the body becomes apparent.
- Heart disease, Croppling, blindness and insanity are possible long-term effects of syphilis.

Once diagnosed, the treatment of syphilis is quite simple, penicillin being still the drug of the first choice.

Mode of Transmission

- Spread during sexual contact with someone who has syphilis.

Consequences if left untreated

- Syphilis can spread to one's sexual partner(s)
- A mother can give it to her unborn baby causing a spontaneous abortion, a neonatal death or birth defects.
- Can cause heart disease, brain and spinal cord damage leading to paralysis, insanity and even death.

Chancroid

Cause: Bacterium (Haemophilus ducreyi)

Symptom

- Small, pain full ulcers on or around the genital organs.
- They tend to grow in size and do not heal by themselves.
- They may even spread to and damage other structures.

Mode of Transmission

- Spread by contact with pus from the ulcers of an infected person during sexual contact.

Consequences if left untreated

- Chancroid can spread to one's sexual partner(s)
- Untreated chancroid can cause painful swelling of the ly ph nodes in the groin but does not lead to permanent damage of the adjacent structures.

Chlamydia

Cause: Bacterium (Chlamydia trachomatis)

Symptoms

- Some men and most women have no symptoms. Those

who do have symptoms show them 7 to 21 days after having sex.

- Burning or pain when urinating
- Pain in the abdomen, sometimes with fever and nausea.

Women

- Discharge from the vagina
- Vaginal bleeding between periods.

Men

- Watery white drip from the penis.

Mode of Transmission

- Spread during sexual contact with someone who has Chlamydia.

Consequences if Left Untreated

- It can spread to one's sexual partner(s)
- A mother can give it to her baby during childbirth causing Pneumonia
- He infection can damage the reproductive organs.
- Both men and women may no longer be able to have children.
- Can cause an ectopic pregnancy. Miscarriage or early delivery of a pregnant women.

CANDIDIASIS:
(ALSO CALLED MONILIASIS OR YEAST INFECTION)

Cause: Fungus (Candida albicans)

Symptoms

Women

- White, curdy, vaginal discharge.
- Vaginal itching
- Vaginal soreness

Men

- Most men have no symptoms.
- Irritation in the penis, particularly the glands.
- Slight rash.
- Discharge from the penis.

Mode of Transmission

- Can spread during sexual contact with someone who has candidiasis.

Consequences if Left Untreated

- It can spread to one's sexual partner(s)
- Inflammation of the vaginal wall.

GRANULOMA INGUINALE: (ALSO CALLED DONOVANOSIS)

Cause: Bacterium (Calymmato bacterium granulomatis)

Symptoms

- Firm, reddish-brown ulcers on the genital organs, anus, buttocks, thighs or face.
- Women may have no symptoms.

Mode of Transmission

- Spread during sexual contact with someone who has granuloma inguinale.

Consequences if left untreated

- It can spread to one's sexual partner(s)
- Untreated granuloma inguinale can spread and block the urethra
- Could result in genital deformities.
- In rare instance, cancer may develop.

Non-Gonococcal Urethritis (NGU) (or Non Specific Urethritis)

Cause

- Have the inflammation of the urethra is not caused by gonorrhea. It may caused by a combination of a virus and a bacterium.

Symptoms

- Most women and some men have no symptoms. Those who do have symptoms show them 1 to 3 weeks after having sex.
- Burning or pain when urinating.

Women

- Discharge from the vagina.

Men

- A yellow or white drip from the penis.

Mode of Transmission

Spread during sexual contact with someone who has non gonococcal urethritis.

Consequences if Left Untreated

- It can spread to one's sexual partner
- A mother can give it to her baby during childbirth.
- The infection can damage the reproductive organs. Both Men and Women may no longer be able to have children.

Trichomoniasis

Cause

- Protozoan (Trichomona vaginalis)

Symptoms

- Most women and some men show no symptoms at all.

Those who do have symptoms show them a few days to a few weeks after having sex.

Mode of Transmission

- Spread during sexual contact with someone who has trichomoniasis

Consequences if Left Untreated

- Trichomoniasis can spread to one's sexual partner
- A mother can give it to her unborn baby
- The infection can damage the reproductive organs. If untreated, men may no longer be able to have any children.

Herpes Genitalis: (also called Genital herpes)

Cause: Virus (Herpes Simplex Virus or HSV)

Symptoms

- Some people have no symptoms. Those who do have symptoms show them 2 to 30 days after having sex, on an average 6 to 7 days.
- Flu-like feelings.
- Small, painful blisters on the genitals, thighs or mouth which last for upto 3 weeks.
- Pain when urinating.
- Itching, burning, pain before the blisters appear.
- Numbness or tingling in buttocks, legs or hips.
- When the blisters burst and then heal the person still has herpes. The blisters can come back, though the recurring attacks are not as severe as the initial one.
- Fever, headache, backache, loss of appetite and general malaise.

Mode of Transmission

- Spread during sexual contact with someone who has herpes (especially during the blister stage)

Consequences if Left Untreated

- Herpes can spread to ones sexual partner
- A mother can give it to her baby during childbirth causing possible brain damage. Therefore, an expectant mother with a herpetic lesion in the vaginal area must undergo a caesarean delivery.
- A mother can give it to her unborn child resulting a spontaneous abortion.
- Herpes cannot be cured. Attacks occur about 3 to 4 times a year for many years. But their intensity gradually decreases.

IV

HIV/AIDS

AIDS stands for:

Acquired	- not born with
Immune	- body's defence system
Deficiency	- not working properly.
Syndrome	- a group of signs and symptoms.

AIDS is not a single disease but a syndrome—a set of diseases, which results from the destruction of the body's defences by the—Human Immunodeficiency Virus, HIV.

Because HIV cause damage to the immune system, the antibodies detected in the blood of the carriers of the HIV are ineffective in halting the damage caused by the virus, which may present in large numbers in the body. Therefore, the body cannot be protected against other infections and cancers, some of which then form the direct causes of death. Because of the way that the virus infects cells, developing a cure or vaccine is extremely difficult.

THE NATURE OF THE VIRUS

The first case of AIDS were recognized in the United States in 1981. The virus that causes it, now called HIV, was first isolated in 1983 at the Institute Pasteur in Paris.

HIV is a member of retrovirus family of viruses which has been known for many years to cause a number of different diseases in animals.

Like all retroviruses, HIV contains RNA in its core; the virus itself is surrounded by a protein and lipid envelope or 'coat'.

HIV selectively infects specific white blood cells (CD4) are an essential part of the body's immune defense system. When the CD4 cells are destroyed, the infected person becomes susceptible to a range of opportunistic infectious diseases and cancers and the group of such condition is called AIDS. HIV may also directly infect nerve cells and cause neurological disorders. HIV takes a long time to cause damage. HIV infection is presumed to be lifelong and the infected person is likely to remain infectious for life.

Cure/Vaccine for AIDS

So far there is no cure for AIDS and a vaccine may be far away. At present, prevention is the only cure for AIDS.

TRANSMISSION

Detailed epidemiological studies throughout the world have documented only THREE modes of Transmission: Sexual, Parental, and Mother to Fetus/Infant.

Side Sexual Transmission

Worldwide, sexual intercourse is the most frequent mode of transmission of HIV. The virus can be transmitted from an infected person to his or her sex partner.

Women are more at risk of getting the infection than men. Because semen contains larger concentrations of HIV than do vaginal fluids, and semen stays for a longer time in the vagina. So also, STD infected persons have a great risk of catching AIDS.

Parenteral Transmission

Parenteral transmission occurs through the transfusion of infected blood products, or the use of blood-contaminated needles, syringes, or other skin-piercing instruments. The risk of acquiring HIV infection is related to the size of the inoculums;

recipients of unit of HIV—infected blood for transfusion have virtually a 100% probability of becoming infected. Transmission through HIV-contaminated needles and syringes is a particularly serious problem among injecting drug users.

Prenatal Transmission

Transmission of HIV infection from a woman to her fetus/infant may occur before, during and after birth. The overall risk of HIV transmission from an HIV-infected woman to her fetus or infant in UTERO or during delivery is 15-39%.

Postnatal transmission through breast milk has been described in a small number of infants of mothers who acquired HIV infection after delivery.

SYMPTOMS OF AIDS

It can take from six months to many years for a person who has been exposed to HIV to develop the disease.

Some people exposed to HIV may never proceed to the final stage of AIDS, but they become "Carriers". Although carriers appear healthy, they can give HIV to a sexual partner or to someone they share a needle with.

The major and minor signs are listed below;

Major Signs

- Weight loss greater than 10% of the body weight.
- Fever for longer than one month.
- Chronic diarrhea for longer than one month (intermittent or consistent)
- Persistent severe fatigue.

Minor Signs

- Persistent cough for longer than one month.
- General itchy dermatitis (skin irritation)
- Recurrent Herpes Zoster (Shingles)

- Oropharyngeal candidiasis (fungus infection in the mouth/throat)
- Chronic progressive and disseminated Herpes Simplex infections.
- General Lymphadenopathy (Swelling of lymph glands)

TESTING AND DIAGNOSIS OF AIDS

Current screening tests do not diagnose AIDS. They detect antibodies to HIV in the blood. The screening test for AIDS is ELISA (Enzyme-linked Immunosorbent Assay) which is the easiest, cheapest and most widely used test. In ELISA, a special electronic instrument measures colour changes in serum when antibodies are exposed to pieces of HIV.

Results from the ELISA test can be confirmed by the more elaborate and expensive Western Blot test.

PREVENTION OF AIDS

There is no satisfactory treatment so far. The picture is gloomy as of today. The only silver lining is that the disease is preventable with simple measures like the promotion of monogamy and fidelity between sexual partners, the use of high quality condoms, the use of sterile needles and syringes, the transfusion of only HIV negative blood and the promotion of *Reproductive Health Education* at the Adolescent stage.

Advantages of Testing Blood for HIV Infection

- Persons who are informed after the best that they do not have HIV infection, would feel relieved.
- People who find out that they have HIV can immediately receive early treatment. If HIV infected people start early treatment, they usually live longer.
- A person with HIV can make decisions to take good care of himself/herself.
- A person can develop a good emotional support system at the early stage of the disease.

- One can utilize new medicines as they develop.
- One can make decisions in respect of child bearing, as babies can be born with HIV, if the mother is HIV positive.
- One can inform his/her partner that he/she has HIV.
- One can abstain from sex or use a condom during sex.
- One can avoid sharing items that come in contact with blood like tooth-brushes, razors, tweezers, needles and syringes.
- A person will decide not to donate blood and other tissues or body organs.
- He/she will practice responsible sexual behaviour.

HIV Transmission in South East Asia

Route of Transmission	*% of Total no. of HIV infected persons*
Sexual intercourse	80-90
Blood Transfusion	3-15
Injecting Drug Use	5-10
Equipment/Needles	0.1
Perinatal (Mother to child)	0.1

QUESTIONS AND ANSWERS

Q. Name three Body Fluids that are Known to Spread the Aids Virus, HIV.

Ans. Male semen, veginal secretions, and blood.

Q. Name the ways in which blood-to-blood transmission of the aids/HIV can occur.

Ans.

- Sharing injection needles and syringes;
- Sharing other instruments—knives, razor blades, tattooing and ear piercing instruments and possibly toothbrushes; blood transfusion.

Q. what are the ways HIV is spread?

Ans. Sexual intercourse; sharing injection needles and syringes and other cutting instruments (i.e. Knives); mother to baby; Blood transfusion.

Q. Give Reasons why Aids is so serious.

Ans.

- No cure for AIDS
- No vaccine to prevent HIV
- Causes death
- Happens to young people
- Discrimination and intolerance.

Q. List the ways that you can protect yourself from HIV and other infection

Ans.

- Not have sexual intercourse
- Delay sex
- Use a condom properly
- Have only one sexual partner who is not infected with HIV/AIDS and has no other sexual partners.
- Do not use dirty injection needles syringes.
- Get injection only at hospitals or health centers.

Q. What is meant by the "window period"? Why is this period so important.

Ans. Window period is the period of time from when a person is infected until antibodies (germ fighters) develop in the blood. This is usually 2 to 12 weeks. It is important because if one is tested during this period, the test will be negative since the test looks for antibodies against HIV, which have not formed yet. However, the person can infect others.

Q. The things a person could do to prevent sexual threats and violence.

Ans.

- Be assertive.
- Avoid secluded (lonely) spots.
- Do not go to person's room if no one else is at home.
- Set sexual limits early
- Do not accept money or presents.
- Do not take rides with strangers.

Q. Give Reasons why it is Important to be Compassionate to a Person with HIV or Aids.

Ans.

- They are often young.

- They are no threat
- They suffer more if isolated
- It is important to think of someone other than yourself
- They will likely die
- It is a painful, long-term disease
- They are often abandoned by family and friends.

Q. What are the ways to be compassionate to a person with HIV or aids?

Ans.

- Write a letter
- Share a meal
- Clean the house
- Give them a hug
- Just listen
- Make a 'fun' present
- Help other family members
- Find others to give support
- Celebrate special days
- Get medicines
- Share emotions-laugh, cry.
- Do not let them blame themselves
- Be friendly
- Play games
- Hold their hand
- Talk about the future

Q. Provide the WYAS that you can give emotional support to people with aids.

Ans.

- Find out about their needs and what they can do for themselves each day
- Share feelings—be honest and open
- Encourage them to do a s much as possible for themselves
- Give support and praise when deserved
- Ask them how they want things done—wash, food, cleaning
- Encourage anger and crying
- Look after yourself—take breaks, ask for help.

TEST ITEMS FOR STUDENTS—TRUE/FALSE (T/F)

1. People with AIDS die from serious illnesses.
2. HIV may be passed from a mother to her unborn child
3. The best method of protection against HIV and STDs is to abstain from sexual intercourse.
4. The birth control pill protects from HIV or STD.
5. AIDS can be cured if you are given medicines early enough.
6. Being compassionate to a person with AIDS is dangeruous because there is good change you will become infected with HIV.
7. People with AIDS should not encouraged to do as much as they can for themselves.
8. People with AIDS, who are upset, should be enbcouraged to cry or be angry.
9. A person who has an STD is at greater risk of getting HIV.
10. Person can have a negative test for HIV and still be infected with HIV.
11. A person to get tested for HIV is so that you will not infect others.
12. There is evidence that HIV can be spread by some type of insects.
13. HIV is found in semen, viginal fluids and blood.
14. Someone with AIDS can spread HIV by coughing and spitting.
15. Once you are infected with HIV, you are infected for life.
16. People infected with HIV do not necessarily look sick.
17. A person can have HIV for years without getting AIDS.
18. Vaccine is available to protect people from HIV infection.
19. You can get HIV by eating food prepared by an HIV infected person.
20. One way to protect yourself from getting HIV is by not having sex.

21. Everyone infected with HIV, whether they have symptoms of AIDS or not, can spread HIV to others.
22. A person may get HIV by donating blood.
23. A person may get HIV by sharing drug needles.
24. You may get HIV by sitting on a toilet seat that a person with AIDS has used.
25. It is not dangerous to hug a person with AIDS.
26. You can't get HIV if you only have sex once or twice without a condom.
27. The more partners a person has, the greater the chances of being infected with HIV.

KEY: 1.T, 2.T, 3.T, 4.F, 5.F, 6.F, 7.T, 8.T, 9.T, 10.T, 11.T, 12.F, 13.T, 14.F, 15.T, 16.T, 17.T, 18.F, 19.F, 20.T, 21.T, 22.F, 23.T, 24.F, 25.T, 26.F, 27. T.

Bibliography

Achmad, Sulistinah Irawati: Westly: Sidney B. 'Indonesian Survey looks at Adolescent Reproductive Health'. Asia—Pacific Population and Policy (51):1-4 October 1999.

Amporsuwanna, et al., 'Case Study Cambodia Communication and Advocacy Strategies' Adolescent Reproductive and Sexual Health. Bangkok: UNESCO PROAP, 2000 p. 37.

Baldo, Mariella, et al., 'Sex Education does not lead to early or Increased Sexual Activity in youth'. Geneva, WHO, GPA, 1992.

Basu D.P., 'Appropriate Methodologies for the Studying Sexual Behavior in India', Indian Journal of Social Work—1974.

Belanger, D. and K.T. Hong. 'Study on Premarital Sex and Abortions of Female youth in Hanoi. UNFPA and Institute of Sociology. 1996.

Berja, Clarinda L. 'Case Study Philippines: Communication and Advocacy Strategies Adolescent Reproductive and Sexual Health'. Bangkok. UNESCO PROAP 1999. p. 29.

Berja, Clarinda. L, 'Case Study on Adolescent and Reproductive and Sexual Health Education in Philippines'. S.I S.N 1999. p. 45.

Bhatia B.D and R. Chandra. 'Adolescent Mother an Unprepared Child', Indian Journal of Maternal and Child Health, 67-70, 1993.

Booklet 2: Advocacy and IEC Programmes and Strategies Bangkok: Communication and Advocacy Strategies: Adolescent Reproductive and Sexual Health. Series one. UNESCO PROAP, 1999, p. 31.

Brander, Carolyn H: 'Older, but not wiser: How men get information about AIDS and sexually transmitted diseases after high school', Family Planning Perspectives. 2000: V32 (1): pp. 33-38.

Byambaa, Enkhtsetseg, 'Case Study, Mongolia: Communication and Advocacy Strategies Adolescent Reproductive and Sexual Health.' Bangkok, 1999, p. 31.

Case study, 'Adolescent Reproductive and Sexual Health Education'. S.I S.N. 1999. p. 43.

Centre wall, Erik, 'Sexuality Education for Adolescents Boys'. Stockholm: Swedish Association for sexed. 1995.

Chandiramani Radhika, 'Talking about Reproductive and Sexual Health Issue with Youth: A Telephone Helpline.' Washington. D.C. Focus on Young Adult (1999). 1 sheet.(Young Adult Reproductive Health Project Highlights).

Chaudhary, R.H., 'Socio Economic Demographic and Reproductive Health Profiles of Adolescents in SAARC countries'. Population and Development in Nepal, Central Department of Population Studies, Tribhuvan University, 1999.

Chehpa, 'Sexual Risk Behavior and Knowledge and Attitude Towards Condom Use and HIV/AIDS Transmission among men in five border towns of Nepal', 1998.

Conger, John, 'Adolescence: Generation under Pressure,' New York—Harper and Row Publishers 1979.

Daniel Ezhilarasu,' Socio Cultural Factors Influencing Promiscuity in Hetro Sexual Males infected with HIV-A Social Study, Unpublished Ph.D Thesis, Dept of Sociology, University Of Madras. 1997.

Department of Family Welfare, 'Reproductive and Child Health Programme'. New Delhi: Ministry of Health and Family Welfare. Government of India. 1997.

Eirhorn, Dorothy, H., 'Adolescence International Encyclopedia of Social Sciences, New York. Free Press. 1982.

Family Planning Association of Srilanka. 'Needs Assessment Study on Sexual Health Education and Services for The Adolescent and Youth in Srilanka': Study Period October 1996. February 1997, p. 83. IPPF Vision 2000.

Farrell, Marguerite., et al, 'Reaching Indigenous Youth with Reproductive Health Information and Services'. Washington, D.C. Focus on Young Adult. 1999, (4) P (In Focus on Young Adults).

Fetters, Tarmara, et al., 'Youth Talk About Sexuality: A Participatory Assessment of Adolescent Sexual and Reproductive Health in Lusaka, Zambia', Lusaka, Zambia, Population Council, 1998, p30.

Flerning C.M. 'Adolescence', London, Rout ledge and Kegan Paul Ltd. 1957.

Flinn. Susan Ki Mariner, David. 'Measuring and Assessing State Policies to Promote Adolescent Sexual and Reproductive Health.' Vol. 1, Washington. D.C. Advocates for Youth, 1998, p. 144.

Foundation for Adolescent Development. 'A Resource Book on Adolescent Health, Sexuality and Development: A Youth to Youth Model'. Manila: Foundation For Adolescent Development: p. 1999-90.

GAO, Ersheng., et al. 'Study on Reproductive Health of Unmarried Youth in China.' China Population Science, 6: 47-54, 1999.

Giang, L. M., and Boarden, L., 'Vietnamese Youth Reproductive Health Needs in the DOI MOI Era.', Population Council: 1998.

Government of India, 'Manual on Family Life Education and Population Education in Schools,' Bombay: Family Planning Training and Research Center 1972 (Mimeo Graphical).

Government of India, Ministry of Human Resource Development of Youth Affairs and Sports, AIDS Education for Student Youth: A Training Manual, New Delhi Government of India 1993.

Gray, Alan and Srisuman Sartsara. 'Case Study Thailand: Communication and Advocacy Strategies Adolescent Reproductive and Sexual Health.' Bangkok. UNESCO PROAP, 1999. p. 26.

Hardjono, Rien, H., et al., Adolescent Reproductive Health For Youth Jakarta, Population Council, 1998, p. 65 (4).

Harmer, Anne. 'The Reproductive Health Situation in Lao PDR with A Focus on Adolescents.' EU/UNFPA Reproductive Health Initiative, SCF (UK) April 1998.

Hirsh, J.S., and Barkes, G., Adolescents and Unsafe Abortion in Developing Countries: A Preventive Tragedy, Washington D.C International Center on Adolescent Fertility, Center for Population Options, 1992.

Hong, K.T, 'Study on Sexuality in Vietnam. The Known and Unknown Issues'. Population Council and Institute of Sociology, Regional Paper No. 11, 1997.

Hughes, Jane, et al. 'Improving the fit adolescents needs and future programmes for sexual and reproductive health in developing countries'. Studies in family planning 29 (2): 234 -242, 1998.

India, National Council of Educational Research and Training, ' Regional Institute of Education. Adolescence Education,' an Awareness Training Package for Secondary Teachers, Mysore, Regional Institute of Education. 1996. IV (Various Paging)

India—National Council of Educational Research and Training Adolescent Reproductive and Sexual Health (Abstract-Bibliography). New Delhi: The Council, (1999). p. 79. (POPDOC Services. Bibliographies Services: NOIDA.)

International Institute for Population Sciences (IIPS), 'National Family and Health Survey 1998-99 India', Bombay IIPS. 2000.

International Institute for Population Sciences (IIPS)' National Family Health Survey (MCH on Family Planning) India and States', (1992-1993), 1995.

Israel, Ronald C et al., 'Promoting Reproductive Health for Younger Adults through Social Marketing and Mass Media a Review of Trends and Practices'. Newton, M.A., Education Development Center. Focus on Young Adults Research Series. 1997, p. 45.

Jejeebhoy, Shireen J., 'Adolescent Sexual Reproductive Behavior: A Review of the Evidence from India.' Washington. D.C. International Center For Research on Women: 1996. p. 35.

Jon khaddar, A.H. 'Training for Sexuality Education HIV/AIDS Prevention'. Paris: UNESCO, 1997.

Karmic Society, Nepal, 'Assessment of Knowledge Attitude and Practice Concerning HIV/AIDS and STD Among Youths in Dang', Kailati assnd Surkhet, 1998.

Khanal, H. 'Adolescent Reproductive Health in Nepal', Journal of Reproductive Health, 45-53, 1999.

Kirby, K.E.S., A Report on Media Content Analysis on Adolescent Reproductive Health Issues in Bhutan. Kuala Lumpur: Asian Institute Development Communication. (1999), p. 24.

Kishore, Attavar, et al., 'Adolescence and Sensibility: Need Assessment of Adolescent Learner's With Regards to Population', SRC, Mysore. 1998.

Lee, Mary Huang Soo. 'Case Study Malaysia: Communication and Advocacy Strategies Adolescent Reproductive and Sexual Health', Bangkok: UNESCO PROAP, 1999, p. 27.

Lee, Mary Huang Soo. Case Study on Adolescent Reproductive and Sexual Health: Malaysia S.I S.N., 1999, p. 45.

Liskin, Lauire, et al., 'AIDS Education—A Beginning Population Reports', Series. L. Number 8, September 1989.

LU, ZIZHI and Yuan Hao. 'Evaluation of Peer Education on AIDS/STI and Safe Sex among College Students- China', Journal of Health Education. 15.5-8.1999.

Ma, Yinghua and Jianping Sun. 'Study and Evolution of Health Education on STI/HIV/AIDS among College Students.' Journal of Chinese School Health, 20: 26-28, 1999.

Madansingh L.M. et al. 'A Study of Adolescent Learners: Knowledge, Attitude and Behavior regarding Gender Equality, Small Family Norms, Reproductive Health, Reproductive Rights. SRC, Lucknow. 1997.

Meekens, Dominique et al., 'Changing Adolescent beliefs about Protective Sexual Behavior': The Botswana Division, Population Service International, 1997, p. 41 (Working Paper: No. 3)

Meekens, Dominique et al., 'Changing Adolescents Beliefs about Protective Sexual Behavior: The Botswana TSA Banana Programme.' Washington, D.C Research Division, and Population Service International. 1997, p. 41 (Working Paper: No 3)

Meekens, Dominique et al., 'Gender Differentials in Adolescent Sexual Activity and Reproductive Health Risks in Cameroon'. Washington. D.C. Population Services International. 1997. 50, (1) P (PSI Research Division Working Paper No 4.

Meekens, Dominique, et al., 'Sexual and Reproductive Health Behavior Among Romanian Adolescents: An Exploratory Narrative Research Analysis. Washington, D.C. Population Services International, 25 (1) P. PSI Research Division. Working Paper No. 11, 1997.

Menseh, Barbara, et al., 'The Changing Social Environment for Adolescent in the Kaggena-Nankana District of Northern Ghana: Implications for Reproductive Behavior' New York 1998-64 (2) P (Working Papers: No. 110)

Mith samlanh. 'KAP Survey on Reproductive Health among Vulnerable Youth'. Phnom Penn. European Union and UNFPA, 1999.

Mngadi, P.T., Faxelid E., Zwane, I.T., Höjer B. & Ransjo-Arvidson A.-B.

'Health providers' perceptions of adolescent sexual and reproductive health care in Swaziland.' *International Nursing Review* 55, 148-155, 2008

Nag, Moni, 'Sexual Behavior and AIDS in India: State of the Art'. The Indian Journal of Social Work, Vol. LV No. 4, October 1994.

Nagarajan N., Kapali, et al., 'A study on awareness of population education among college students', PERC, Department of Adult and Continuing Education, University of Madras. 1998

Nagarajan, N., 'A study of knowledge and Attitude to sexuality and Reproductive health among the college Adolescents in Tamil Nadu'. Indian Journal of population Education, No. 18. September 2002.

Nagarajan, N., 'A study on knowledge and attitude on sexuality, STDs and HIV/AIDS among the college Adolescent' The EDUCATIONAL REVIEW, Vol. 44. No. 6, June 2001.

Nagarajan, N., 'Adolescent Reproductive Health Education: Need for social Development' in the life long learning for social development: A Review of Global perspectives. The University of Nigmagan. The Netherlands. 2002.

Nagarajan. N 'Women's status and role in population education' Indian Journal of Adult and continuing Education, April-June, 1992.

Nagarajan. N. 'Constraints in containing population growth' International Journal of Ideas: THIRD CONCEPT. No. 138, August, 1998.

Nakron Pattern, Institute for Population and Social Research, Mahidol University 1999. p. 36.

National Resource Center for Non Formal Education, Nepal. 'Case Study. Nepal Communication And Advocacy Strategies Adolescent Reproductive And Sexual Health'. Bangkok. UNESCO PROAP 2000, p. 30.

National University of Mongolia, 'Population Teaching and Research Center Adolescent Reproductive and Sexual Health: Case Study In Mongolia Ulaanbaatar'. Population Teaching and Research Center 1999. p. 45.

NCERT, 'Adolescence Education: Report of the National Seminar', New Delhi. NCERT. 1994.

Nga, Q.L. and Hong, K.T., 'Adolescent Reproductive Health: Baseline survey in Honoi', Vinh Ph.D and Thai Binn'. Ministry of Health. 1997.

Ngnyen Quoc Anh et al., 'Adolescent Reproductive Health: Survey and Assessment of Knowledge, Attitude and Practice of Adolescents in Hai Phong City about Reproductive Health Issues. Honoi', National Community for Population and Family Planning, 1999, p. 62.

Ngo, Vonrarath, Saysavanth, 'Case Study Lao PDR Communication and Advocacy Strategies Adolescent Reproductive and Sexual Health', Bangkok: UNESCO PROAP 2000. p. 23.

Nhan, V.Q., NDM Hang, et al., 'Reproductive Health Behavior of

Unmarried Urban Students of Age 17-24 in Vietnam'. National Committee for Population and Family Planning (NCPEP) and Center for Population Study and Information (CPSI) 1996.

Panchaud, Christine, et al., 'Sexually Transmitted Disease among Adolescents in Developing Countries'. Family Planning Perspectives. 2000. V 32 (1) pp. 24-32.

Pandey, Jawaharlal, et al., 'Adolescence Education: Knowledge Base New Delhi: Department of Education in Social and Humanities'. National Council of Educational Research and Training 1999, p. 84 (Adolescent Education in Schools).

Pathak, K.B. and F. Ram. 'Adolescent Motherhood: Problems and Consequences'. Journal of Family Welfare 39 (1): 17-23. 1993

Population Council-Hanoi. 'Report on the Second Training Course on Sexuality and Communication Skill for Local Staff.' Project Soccer and HIV/AIDS 1998.

Quackenbush, Marcia, et al. 'The HIV Challenge: Prevention Education for Young People'. 2nd Ed. Santa Cruz, CAETR, Associates, 1995, p. 547.

Quan, Le Nga. 'Case Study Vietnam: Communication and Advocacy Strategies Adolescent Reproductive and Sexual Health.' Bangkok. UNESCO PROAP 2000, p. 36.

Radhakrishnana, et al. 'Identification the Inter Section: Adolescent Unwanted Pregnancy, HIV/AIDS and Unsafe Abortion'. Carrboro, N.C., IPAS, 1997, p. 20.

Raga van Gilbert, Praema. 'Adolescent Reproductive Health: Issues and Challenges: S.I., S., 1998, p. 6.

Rahim, Samsudin A. 'The Role of Mass Media Practices in Promoting Adolescent Reproductive and Sexual Health Issues'. Module-1 Kulalumbur. Asian Institute For Development Communication 1999, p. 27.

Ram, F. and Sanjay Mohanty, 'Reproductive and Child Health Status in India: District Level Analysis of RHS', International Institute for Population Sciences, Mumbai 1998.

Reproductive Health Association of Cambodia. 'Adolescent Reproductive Health Survey: A Baseline Study of School Going Adolescent In Phnom Penn.' Phnom Penn 1999.

Sali kumar, P.N., 'A determinants of Fertility in Rural Areas. A Study of Selected Villages in Kanyakumari District, Tamil Nadu. India', Unpublished Ph.D. Thesis. Dept. of Economics University of Madras, 1992.

Senderowitz, Judith, 'Reproductive Health Outreach Programmes for Young. Washington. D.C. Focus on Young Adults. 1997.55p (Research Services).

Senderowitz, Judith, 'Young People and STDs/HIV/AIDS: Part III

Programme To Address The Problem', Washington D.C. (In Focus on Young Adults) 1997.

Senderowitz, Judith. 'Young People and STDs/HIV/AIDS, PART- I. Dimension of The Problem.' Washington D.C. 1997, (4) P (In Focus: Focus On Young Adults).

Shad Pour, K. 'Case Study Iran: Communication and Advocacy Strategies Adolescent Reproductive and Sexual Health'. Bangkok, UNESCO PROAP 1999, p. 19.

Shadpour, K.A., 'Report on Adolescent Reproductive and Sexual Health Education in the Islamic Republic of Iran. Tehran', Iran, Ministry of Health and Medical Education. 1999, p. 37.

Shafeqa, Fathimah, 'Case Study, Maldives Communication and Advocacy Strategies Adolescent Reproductive and Sexual Health'. Bangkok: UNESCO PROAP 2000, p. 29.

Shah, Kanul, et al,. 'Listening to Young Voices: Facilitating Participatory Appraisals on Reproductive Health With Adolescent. Lusaka, Zambia', Care International, Zambia. Focus Tool Series 1. 1999, p. 88.

Sharma R.C. 'Case Study: India. Communication and Advocacy Strategies Adolescent Reproductive and Sexual Health'. Bangkok: UNESCO PROAP 2000. p. 34.

Singh, Madan Sing, L.M, et al. 'A Study of Adolescent Learner's Knowledge, Attitude and Behavior Regarding Gender Equality Small Family Norms Reproductive Health and Reproductive Rights'. Lucknow: Literacy House, State Resource Center. UP. 1998, p. 97.

Solim, Ly, Catherine, et al., 'Young People: HIV, STDs and Sexual Health Project. Survey of Knowledge, Attitudes and Practices Phonon Penn.' Save The Children Find (OK) Cambodia (1997).

Styeos, J., Mayone. 'Adolescent Attitude towards Family Size in India: The Impact of Gender, Culture, and Values'. New York. Department of Rural Sociology, Cornell University. 1998, p. 14 (Working Paper Series: No 98-04).

Sun, Jiangping,' Case Study China Communication and Advocacy Strategies: Adolescent and Reproductive and Sexual Health, Bangkok: UNESCO, PROAP 2000, p. 26.

Suprite Bezbaruah, Mondeep K. Janeja, 'Asolescents in India. A profile', Inter Agency Working Group Population and Development, September 2000.

Suresh. M. Jayakumar babu. 'A socio cultural analysis of AIDS patients in Madras Metropolitan area'. Unpublished M.Phil thesis. Dept of Geography, Presidency College Madras. 1994.

Termin, Miriam, J., et al.: 'Perception of Sexual Behaviour and Knowledge about Sexual Transmitted Diseases among Adolescents in Benin City,' Nigeria'. International Family Planning Perspectives. V. 25 (4) pp. 186-190.

The South Asia Conference. 'The South Asia Conference on Adolescents. New Delhi, India 21-23 July 1998 Kathmandu, UNFA, CST For CASA, 1999, p. 69.

Uddin, Nassir, 'Case Study Bangladesh: Communication and Advocacy Strategies Adolescent Reproductive and Sexual Health', Bangkok: UNESCOPROAP, 1999, p. 31.

Umamaheshwari, M. 'Role of Voluntary Health Organizations in Health Care With Special Reference to Voluntary Health Services, Chennai'. Unpublished Ph.D Thesis, Department of Politics and Public Administration. University of Madras. 2001.

UNAID. 'Impact of HIV and Sexual Health Education and the Sexual Behavior of Young People'. A Review Updated. UNAIDS Best Practice Collection, 1997.

UNESCO Principal Regional Office for Asia and Pacific. 'The Population and Education Communication: Booklet-3. Lessons Learned and Guidelines. Regional Clearing House, Bangkok. UNESCO PROAP, 1999-18 p. (Communication And Advocacy Strategies Adolescent Reproductive and Sexual Health Series One).

UNESCO Principal Regional Office For Asia and The Pacific. Regional Clearing House on Population Education and Communication.

UNESCO, 'Family Life Education: Package one, Bangkok, UNESCO, Principle Regional office for Asia and The Pacific, Population Education Programmes Series, 1988.

UNESCO, 'Population Education in Non-Formal Education And Development Programmes—A Manual For Field Workers', Bangkok: UNESCO, Regional Office For Education in Asia and The Pacific, Population Education Programme Service, 1981.

UNFPA, ' Responsible Sexual and Reproductive Health Behavior among Adolescents', South Asia Conference on the Adolescents (July—21-23, 1998) New Delhi, India 1998.

UNFPA, 'Programme of Action of The International Conference on Population and Development', 1996.

UNFPA. 'A Time between Health, Sexuality and Reproductive Rights of Young People'. New York UNFPA: 1999, p. 24.

Valley Researchers Group, 'A Study on Adolescents Sexual and Reproductive Behavior: Cross-Section Analysis', 1998.

Villanueva, Carmelita. L. 'Adolescent Reproductive and Sexual Health Education in School Curricula: Gaps and Opportunities for East and South East Asia'. Bangkok. UNESCO, 1998.

Vulnerability and opportunity, 'Adolescents and HIV/AIDS in The Developing World: Findings from The Women and AIDS Research Programme'. Washington. D.C. International Center for Researcher on Women. 1996. 24 p.

WHO, 'The Reproductive Health of Adolescents—A Strategy for Action',

Geneva: World Health Organization. 1989.

WHO, 'Understanding and Living With AIDS ', New Delhi: World Health Organization, Regional Guide To HIV And AIDS In India. Bombay, Popular Pakistan Pvt. Ltd., 1994.

WHO. 'A Study of The Sexual Experiences of Young People in Eleven African Countries', Geneva, WHO. 1992.

WHO/UNFPA/UNICEF, 'The Reproductive Health of Adolescents: A Strategy For Action', Geneva, WHO 1989.

Xi, and Sujian. An Investigation on College Student Attitude and Behaviors in China', Journal of Health Education. 1999:15:39-41.

Yakandawala Y.L.H. and Swarna Ranathunga. 'Case Study: Srilanka. Communication and Advocacy Strategies—Adolescent Reproductive and Sexual Health'. Bangkok: UNESCO PROAP 1999. p. 33.

Young Lives at Risk: Adolescents and Sexual Health. London, Panos. Institute 1999. p. 22. (Panos Briefing: No. 35)

Index